It Only Took a Moment

By

Regina Venturella

I0084886

It Only Took a Moment

Author: Regina Venturella

Editors: Edward Nasello
            Michael Aubele

Cover photographs contributed by Janine Camp, Emily Nasello, and the Economy Borough Police Department.

Cover design by Edward Nasello.

To contact the author of this book, you may send an email to: rlventurella@verizon.net

Library of Congress Control Number: 2011903437

ISBN 10: 0-615-45703-7
ISBN 13: 978-0-615-45703-1

Acknowledgements

First, the greatest thanks goes to God Almighty, without Him nothing is possible and with Him all is possible.

To everyone who heard our story and hopped on the prayer train and bombarded heaven with your prayers—a heartfelt thank you.

Also, thanks to all of the angels God placed in our way along this difficult journey. The doctors, nurses, therapists, and anyone involved in the care or treatment of Alisha.

Thank you to Michael Aubele for answering the phone at the Valley News Dispatch and offering to help me with the process of writing this book and encouraging me when I was down.

While in Florida, a chance encounter led me to meeting Eddie Nasello, an author of educational books. He had just finished his latest book titled *In Their Own Words: The Wisdom and Passion of Our Founding Fathers*. He was instrumental in the final editing of my book and assisting in getting it to print.

The concept for the book cover design was contributed by my nursing classmate and friend for 48 years, Jane Dallara.

A huge "thank you" to our family and friends. They were the glue that held me together when I was sure I was coming apart. For their shoulders that I cried on and the support they provided, I will forever be grateful.

Table of Contents

Foreword

I firmly believe that when we are born, God has a plan for each of us. In His infinite wisdom, He gave us a free will to make our own choices—sometimes we make good ones, other times we make bad ones.

As we travel the road of life, we may come to learn how one bad choice can have catastrophic consequences. In the case of my family, it left us asking "Why didn't she buckle up?"

Most of us wish we had "do-overs," but we learn early on, that is not possible. The best we can do, is learn from our mistakes, help others to learn, and try never to make the same error in judgment again.

Even though I worked as a registered nurse for over 22 years, I never had to provide care for a patient with a TBI (traumatic brain injury).

Like most people, I was familiar with the unfortunate consequences of serious brain injury from hearing about soldiers who were wounded during battle and athletes who had sustained permanent brain damage from participation in contact sports such as football. But I had no firsthand knowledge of how life-changing a serious brain injury could be—until the accident.

No one among our circle of family or friends would have chosen this journey, but it is the one we must travel and do the best we can.

My purpose in keeping a journal and telling our family's story is to help others—to spread hope where there is none, belief where there is doubt, and encouragement in the face of tragedy.

Chapter 1

It Only Took a Moment

For the better part of a month, we listened from inside the hushed environment of our self-imposed prison to the sound of an emergency medical helicopter taking off and landing. Each trip it made potentially meant a situation as horrific and dire as ours. We knew when it descended on the helipad it wouldn't be long before another grieving family joined us, forced to endure the uncertainty that comes with having a loved one rushed to one of Pittsburgh's trauma centers.

During the 24 days my family and I spent in the Allegheny General Hospital trauma unit waiting room, we witnessed injury and illness inflicted on young and old alike. Among some of those flown in were a 15-year-old boy and an 18-year-old woman injured in separate car accidents; a man suffering from a flesh-eating bacteria; a woman who contracted a blood infection that resulted in the amputation of her arm and leg; a man beaten and left for dead; and a gunshot victim kept under police guard day and night.

And then there was my granddaughter, 19-year-old Alisha Webb, who arrived the morning of February 4, 2009, after wrecking her car in Baden—a quiet southwestern Pennsylvania town about 20 miles northwest of Pittsburgh. Lish, as our family and friends like to call her, drove over a patch of black ice along Conway Wallrose Road while on her way to morning classes at Community College of Beaver County. She lost control of her 2000 Mercury Sable on a bend and crossed the line dividing the winding, two-lane road. An oncoming SUV struck the passenger side of her car, mangling it into a crumpled mess. When I heard of the accident, I thought, "Was someone killed?" Thank God, the other driver walked away from the accident with a broken finger; there were no fatal injuries. I am grateful to this woman for calling 911 to report the accident. I sometimes think of us meeting and talking about that day.

Unfortunately, Lish, who wasn't wearing her seat belt, wasn't left unscathed.

Economy Ambulance, which was the closest ambulance company, received the call for her accident at 7:55 A.M.—five minutes before shift change. In addition, members of the Baden and Economy volunteer fire departments also responded.

Two people who worked on the ambulance crew were employed by the department, the rest of the men and women, were volunteers.

It is said, "God works in mysterious ways." That proved to be so very true the morning of Lish's accident.

One of the employees, a registered nurse, told us he loved working on the ambulance crew so very much. He was able to accomplish this by putting in two to three 24 hour shifts at the department, and supplementing it with a day or two in the local hospital emergency room.

Even though he was off duty that day, when the call came in, he said he felt compelled to respond. Something inside of him made him go. His expertise proved invaluable in Lish's initial care. The skills he possessed enabled him to quickly evaluate her and determine the level of care she required.

The nurse and other emergency responders who turned out that morning agreed to speak with me about the accident about a year after it happened to help me recollect the events as accurately as possible. They agreed as a group not to have their names printed, saying it had to do with the true spirit of volunteerism.

Those who arrived first the morning of the accident said they found Lish lying face-down with her head against the passenger-side door and her feet tangled in the steering wheel. Her left shoulder had gotten wedged under the glove compartment, and her right shoulder rested on the front passenger seat. Aside from being unresponsive, she showed no signs of external injuries, such as bleeding, cuts or bruises.

One of the firefighters who helped extricate Lish said, "Her face has been seared into my mind forever." He said it was the first time in 19 years he had ever heard such loud "snoring respirations." He could tell she was definitely in respiratory distress.

Knowing they had little time to waste, the crew members extricated Lish in 8 minutes. They all pitched in and quickly removed the shattered front window, the rear window and both side doors. One EMT climbed in through the back and helped to support Lish's head and neck as the others got her out. They placed her on the stretcher, anchored her neck with a brace, made certain her airway was open and placed her gently into the ambulance.

By 8:23 A.M., they left the scene, and headed for the closest hospital, which was in Sewickley.

They had called LifeFlight, but were told the helicopter was unable to fly due to inclement weather. The EMTs had recognized she needed to be stabilized before making the trip into Pittsburgh. They knew she suffered a serious head injury because she was extremely combative, despite being unconscious. They understood that any indication of a head injury needs to be treated immediately and taken very seriously. On the way, they inserted an IV access line and hung a bag of normal saline.

They made a quick stop at Heritage Valley Sewickley Hospital. Lish's airway was made patent by intubating her, she was given medication to stabilize her vital signs and then driven to AGH (Allegheny General Hospital) with sirens blaring.

Our family considers the first responders heroes, but they refuse to think of themselves as such. "We are just tools in God's tool box." they said.

As a nurse, I know it only takes a moment for someone's life to change. I had seen it throughout my career; people having strokes, heart attacks, surgeries and dealing with the aftermath of complications following .

The initial response in someone's care can make all the difference in the outcome.

The police identified Lish from the business card in her wallet, which had her father's name on it. It read: TFC Stanford A. Webb, 111 Pennsylvania State Police. A police chief at the scene of the accident called the phone number on the card and reached Stan's friend, Cpl. Kevin L. Brown. Kevin was on duty that morning as the shift supervisor. When the police chief informed Kevin of the circumstances of the crash, Kevin knew immediately it was Lish.

Kevin had first met Stan and Lish's mother, Janine Camp, at Indiana University of Pennsylvania. He remembered seeing Lish when she was young—about 1 year old. He thought she was an adorable baby and had heard from Stan what a beautiful young lady she had become.

Upon hearing the news, Kevin immediately contacted Stan by cell phone and proceeded to give him directions to the hospital emergency room. He then contacted hospital security to alert them of Stan's arrival and secured a parking space for him. After taking care of that, he drove immediately to the hospital and arrived in 20 minutes.

Kevin watched from outside a privacy curtain as hospital staff treated Lish. He felt extremely nervous about the situation because he could tell by all of the activity that Lish was in trouble. He said his chief thought, which he hated to entertain, was—*she may not survive.*

As soon as Stan arrived, Kevin filled him in on Lish's condition and escorted him to his beautiful daughter.

At their Baden home only a few miles away from the accident scene, Janine and her husband, Steve Camp, had just gotten Lish's stepbrother, Steven, and stepsister, Alexis, off to school when the phone rang.

Not so long ago, Janine had kissed Lish goodbye as she left for her classes. Knowing Lish had a Spanish exam that day, Janine wished her luck and said she would see her later. Janine and Steve were in the middle of their morning routine when the call came in.

Steve answered, and almost immediately, Janine could sense that something was wrong with Lish.

Janine recounted the shock and distress:

> *"I kept asking Steve what was wrong. When he told me to hang on, I ran upstairs and grabbed the other phone; it was the police. I frantically asked if she was OK. The police explained to me that Lish had been in a car accident and that they were taking her to AGH from the hospital in Sewickley. I instantly knew things weren't good. AGH is a major trauma center. I wondered why they just couldn't take care of her at Sewickley."*

Janine dressed and left for the hospital by herself. The furnace broke that morning, forcing Steve to stay behind with their youngest son, Anthony, to wait for the repairman.

Pure fear drove Janine to pray. She could recall—

> *"I remember asking the Lord to please protect her—to take care of her. Then, I began to thank him. 'Thank you Lord. Thank you Jesus,' I repeated. I knew he would help my baby."*

While driving, Janine called her brothers to relay the news. Unable to reach them, she left messages.

In the middle of the trip, while stuck in traffic, she forgot how to get to the hospital. Her mind went totally blank. Janine described the event:

> *"I had driven to that area many times. Why I couldn't remember how to get there, I don't know."*

Knowing we needed to hear the news and her dad could offer directions, she called us.

My husband Jim and I were vacationing at our second home outside Orlando. We had recently fulfilled a lifelong dream by purchasing a home for us and our family to retreat to in the cold months of winter.

Jim and I were enjoying a lazy morning, hoping to spend a relaxing day at the pool. I had just poured a cup of tea and was sitting down to watch my favorite soap opera, The Guiding Light. Jim was on the porch reading the paper and drinking a cup of coffee when the phone rang.

Jim, who earlier that morning fielded a call from Janine's husband about their furnace problems, answered the phone thinking it was Steve. Instead, he heard Janine crying uncontrollably. He couldn't grasp where she was or what had gone wrong.

"Lish has been in a bad accident," Janine kept repeating. "They're taking her to AGH. I'm on my way there now."

As soon as I overheard this end of the conversation, I became alarmed.

Jim struggled to understand more of what she was trying to say. The only thing that was clear was that she needed directions and help finding the right highway exit.

"Don't worry," Jim told her, using a remarkably collected tone. "You won't know how severe it is until you get there."

After several wrong turns, somehow, she found the correct exit, located a parking space and rushed into the emergency room. She had tears streaming down her cheeks, and her hands were shaking.

Jim and I were in agony awaiting some news. I put in a call to both of our sons, Jimmy and John, asking them to call the minute they knew anything.

Several hours passed when Jimmy called his dad after seeing Lish. He said, "It doesn't look good, dad."

Jim told his son that he and I would be flying home that evening. He told Jimmy that he planned on leaving the car at the airport. Jimmy said, "Dad, you need to get a ride to the airport, you won't be able to return to Florida for quite awhile." At that point, Jim became extremely concerned and worried.

Being a very quiet man, Jim said little, but his face spoke volumes.

What transpired between getting the awful call and flying home that evening, I remember little. Somehow, I was able to book our flight, pack, get dressed and get in touch with Monica, our youngest son John's fiancée. Beyond that, I recall one thing about that day: a sense of overwhelming panic—one our entire family experiences again when we think or talk about the accident.

When we arrived at the Greater Pittsburgh Airport, it was after midnight. The place seemed deserted. The stores and restaurants were all closed. No passengers could be seen waiting at their gates to depart. Very few employees were at their posts.

We hurried to baggage claim, so as not to waste a minute. Jimmy was waiting for us there. We embraced and went to his car.

On the way home, I asked him to stop at the hospital. He said we wouldn't be able to see Lish as there were strict visiting hours. I still wanted to stop and see Janine, but he said, "Mom, you and dad need to get a good night's sleep."

We arrived home after 2 A.M.

Neither Jim nor I could sleep. We tried to talk, but didn't know what to say. All we could do was hold onto each other and pray that all would be OK.

Anxious to get to the hospital, we showered and left before daybreak. On the way, we passed a billboard we had never noticed before. It featured one word: BELIEVE. We knew immediately God was sending us a message—a very strong message we fought desperately to hold onto.

Jim and I arrived at the hospital at 6 A.M. to find Janine and Stan camped out in one corner of the waiting room. We ran to them and embraced. Janine began crying and Stan had tears in his eyes as well.

They both started to explain what they knew about the accident and Lish's condition. Jim and I couldn't stop crying as we listened. The report almost took us to our knees.

As I have mentioned, as a nurse, I knew it only takes a moment for someone's life to change. I have witnessed it. Now I was beginning my own journey, the ending yet to be known.

Chapter 2

Not Even a Thread

At the time I first sat down to begin writing this book, it had been more than a year since that dreadful day. To help with the challenging task, I began by asking Janine and other family members to recount for me their memories of the experience. In doing so, we noticed that some of our memories of the way things played out differed. But the crucial part remained constant—each of us was stricken with great fear because of how much we love Lish and the uncertainty of what was to come.

Janine shared with me what she remembered about the first stress filled moments at the hospital:

> "When I got to the emergency room, I gave them my name and told them who I needed to see. The receptionist told me to stay in the waiting area and that a social worker would be out to see me. 'I need to see my daughter,' I demanded. 'Is she OK?'
>
> "The receptionist repeated herself, telling me to remain in the waiting area and that a social worker would be out. By that response, I knew things weren't good. At that point, I began to cry. All I wanted was to see my baby and hold her. I was only a set of doors away."

As it turned out, John's fiancée Monica rushed into the emergency room before the social worker came out to talk to Janine.

Monica recalled the events with chilling clarity:

> "I ran to Janine and heard a sound I'd never heard before. I believed it was the sound of a mother's heart when it was wounded beyond repair. Janine was barely able to speak to me, so I filled the silence between sobs with

words of encouragement that I wasn't even sure I believed."

Before even getting to see Janine, Monica knew the situation was serious. She said her anxiety level had almost reached a tipping point before she walked into the emergency room.

She continued telling the events as she recalled:

"I arrived there only to be greeted by a metal detector and an employee who required me to turn over my purse to be searched. I was angry. All I wanted to do was get to Janine and Alisha.

"When I finally passed the inspection, I asked for help at the desk. If you have ever been to the emergency room to visit someone whose injury is beyond serious, you'll understand this—When I mentioned that I was a family member of Alisha Webb's, the receptionist looked at me with such sad eyes that I feared the worst. I had never had anyone look at me like that before; like she was truly terrified about what I was about to find out."

When the social worker finally appeared, he took Janine and Monica into a conference room to explain what happened to Lish.

He began by telling them that she was in a car accident and was in critical condition. After that, Janine could not remember a word that the social work said. All she wanted was to see her daughter.

When Janine was finally permitted to see her daughter, her immediate reaction was: *She doesn't look that bad.*

Janine shared her recollection of those first few moments after seeing her daughter for the first time since the accident:

"It was when I started questioning what all of the tubes were for that the severity of her injuries set in. I'm not sure if it was a doctor or nurse who said it, but someone told me Alisha wasn't breathing and needed to be put on life support. They said she had slipped into a coma."

Janine's brother Jimmy was in a monthly information technology clinical strategy meeting when he saw a message from me at about 10 A.M. When he finished the meeting—and while walking to his next one—he listened to the message.

In that message, I informed him about the accident and how upset his sister was. I told him no one knew the seriousness of Lish's injuries.

Jimmy was about to make his way to the hospital and assured me he would call as soon as he knew anything.

Each of Jimmy's coworkers expressed concern, told him to drive carefully and to keep them informed.

Jimmy recounted the experience:

"I was in shock. I had great concern and became flustered trying to get my briefcase and get to the hospital as soon as possible."

Despite his anxiety and knowledge that things could be very bad, in his heart, he believed everything would turn out OK.

Jimmy arrived at the hospital about half an hour after getting my call. A member of the hospital staff escorted him to where Lish was being treated.

Inside the room with Lish, the doctors and nurses asked everyone to scream Alisha's name to try to wake her up. One doctor explained that people will sometimes respond to a familiar voice. But after several minutes, everyone was told to stop.

The doctors and nurses had also asked Janine and Jimmy to hold down Lish's arms, which were thrashing about.

Janine could remember vividly—

> *"She was so strong. I remember using both of my arms and all the strength I had to try to restrain her right arm. I looked at Jimmy, and he was struggling as well. He said to me, 'I can't believe how strong she is.'"*

Janine was forced to have Jimmy take in all the names and information that the doctors and nurses were telling them. She knew she was incapable of comprehending anything being said.

John arrived a little later, and said of his first glimpse of Lish:

> *"I couldn't believe my eyes. It kicked me into a state of shock and disbelief. I felt as though I was in a bad dream. Lish looked OK physically—no cuts, blood or obvious injuries—although she was hooked up to all sorts of tubes and equipment."*

Reality set in for John as the doctors began describing the severity of her injuries. He realized how important it would be for him to remain strong for his sister.

The two main things that kept running through John's mind were be strong for Janine and to hold onto to his faith in God.

He kept telling himself that God would take care of Alisha. He knew she was in God's hands and would be all right.

Lora, Jimmy's wife, was also among the first to learn about Lish's accident. She could recall—

> *"I had gone to the gym to teach one class. Sometimes I think to check the phone for messages, other times I don't. That morning I did check and when I saw seven new messages, I felt, 'Oh-No!' something is wrong. I sat down and pressed play. The first message was from Janine, her words were clear, but I heard hysteria. The next was from my husband, Jim. Several came from my mother- and father-in-law. The rest were additional messages from my husband.*
>
> *"I rushed to the hospital."*

Before my husband and I were able to see our granddaughter the morning we arrived at the hospital, the primary neurosurgeon met our family in the waiting room. He informed everyone that the immediate prognosis was grim. He said it was uncertain if Lish would survive and, if she did, there would be no way of knowing what quality of life she would have.

Speaking matter-of-factly, the doctor told us that Lish endured a traumatic brain injury. He said she suffered a diffuse axonal injury that involved damage to the nerve cells in her brain and the loss of connections among those neurons. He also said she had multiple spots of bleeding throughout the brain, and the three spots of blood on the brain stem were of dire concern.

In addition, he said Lish had a ruptured spleen that might need to be removed, a heart contusion and multiple neck fractures.

This doctor spoke to us in an extremely condescending manner. When we asked him to spell a medical term he had just mentioned, he spelled it out indignantly:

"D i f f u s e — A x o n a l — I n j u r y."

Jimmy questioned what he could research on the internet. To that, the doctor responded, "Don't waste your time."

We all looked at one another, but no one knew what to say.

We were each trying to process the news we had just been given or should I say, punched in the gut with.

Most upsetting for our family was knowing we couldn't talk with Lish. We couldn't take her into our arms and hold her or comfort her, the way we wanted to, with all of the lifesaving equipment she was attached to. Lish had slipped into a deep coma.

We were left with nothing to do but wait, hope and pray.

Chapter 3

Bound by Sorrow

During the time we spent huddled in our corner of the waiting room, watching other families come and go, we wondered what each update would bring.

Cold and barren, the waiting room offered families little in the way of hominess or comfort, other than keeping us as close to our loved ones as possible. The carpet was threadbare and the walls a drab beige. The furniture was old, stained and uncomfortable. In the middle of the room, which was about 60 feet by 60 feet, there was a small space that held a coffee pot and a vending machine.

Every family staked out some space—some in the corners, some along the walls and others in the center of the room. Everybody kept their belongings neatly around their camp site.

Family and friends brought in snacks, water, toiletries and blankets and pillows.

Janine assessed it this way:

> *"It was like nothing I'd ever experienced before. It was filled with old, sometimes broken furniture. They had the chairs lined up against the walls with a few loveseats and several round tables. And there was an old TV mounted high in the center of the room. The TV controller was long gone, so someone needed to mount a chair to change the channel."*

Bright overhead lights remained lit both night and day. Everyone tried to find the switch to dim them, but no one was successful.

After so much time, Janine found peace in the waiting room:

"I found comfort there when I would close my eyes. I could

picture a vivid image of a print I saw in an emergency room in Florida several years prior. It was a picture of a doctor sitting at his desk with Jesus standing behind him, resting his hand on the doctor's shoulder. The title was, 'The Great Physician.'

"I knew Alisha wasn't in her room alone. Jesus was there with her every second and He was taking care of her. I didn't know how to make Alisha better, but I knew Jesus was and is our Great Healer. All of my trust was in Him."

She felt it was never easy leaving that room, whether it was to use the restroom or go to the cafeteria to eat. There was always a family member in the waiting room, and she had her cell phone connected to her hip ... just in case.

The waiting room contained two phones—one for outgoing calls and the other an internal line to reach the families, who were waiting for updates. Every time the internal line rang, someone would run to answer it while the other families waited anxiously to see who was being called. One never knew if it would be bad news.

There were only two windows in the room, and we managed to set up camp in the far left corner under one of them. We placed our pictures of Lish on the window sill and stacked our pillows and blankets and a cooler filled with water against the wall.

When one of Lish's girlfriends brought in flowers, we put them on a low table we found. Janine and I did everything we could to make it seem less like a waiting room and more like a sitting area.

The corner our family carved out contained a small, two-seater chair, a straight-back chair, and a recliner, which Lish's father took from another area of the hospital. Standing 6 feet 8 inches, and wearing his police uniform, I guess no one wanted to tell him he couldn't confiscate it.

Outside the window sat the helipad. The helicopter took off and landed at all hours of the day and night.

The nurses were very kind. Every night after visiting hours were over and only the families were left in the waiting room, they would permit Janine to go back between 10 P.M. and 11 P.M. to say goodnight to Lish. It would only be for a few minutes, but she looked forward to that time. She would hold her, say some prayers, kiss her goodnight and turn on her CD player with the same healing scriptures she was listening to in the waiting room. She treasured those moments.

Stan stayed with Janine that first night. After sharing with us all he knew about Lish and the accident, he then mentioned he was dealing with severe neck pain. I could tell he had the classic signs of an infection. His neck was red, warm and swollen. I advised him to see his doctor.

Several hours later, he called Janine from Butler Memorial Hospital. He was admitted with a staph infection and was on IV antibiotics. He had an infected hair follicle on the back of his neck.

Obviously, we were concerned for Stan. But, his staph infection increased our concern for Lish. She had several access points for the bacteria to enter: A tube for breathing, several IV lines and a foley catheter. Unknowingly, Stan had leaned over her and kissed her during the times he was permitted to see her.

The doctors were also concerned, and reinforced that everyone must use the proper hand washing technique when entering and leaving the trauma unit.

Thankfully, Lish never contracted a staph infection.

I vividly recall the first night I stayed at the hospital. The nurse caring for Lish encouraged us to leave. Janine and I would hear none of it.

The nurse also said she wasn't permitted to give out pillows and blankets. But, she eventually gave in, returning about an hour later with one pillow and two sheets, instructing us to make sure they were returned.

I used my coat as a pillow and curled up on the two-seater. Janine tried to sleep in the recliner. We rested, but neither of us could sleep. There was way too much activity in the waiting room.

The next day, some family members and a group of Lish's closest friends started arriving in a steady stream. Some of our family members brought in pillows and blankets, which we felt compelled to share with the other families huddled in their sections of the room.

We were able to form friendships with some of the others who were forced into situations similar to ours. We shared our stories and grief, prayed together and formed a bond through sorrow and anguish.

So many families came and went. There were several Janine said she'll never forget.

One night, she and her husband were sitting in their corner of the waiting room. Another husband and wife sat at a nearby table. It was about 11 P.M. when a doctor and a nurse came out from the patient area. They sat down with the couple and said, "We did everything we could, but she didn't make it."

As soon as Janine heard this, she just began to cry. Even though she didn't know the couple, her heart just melted.

Within minutes of the exchange with the doctor and nurse, the husband approached Janine, who expressed her sympathy. He said it was OK. He told them it was his mother who died. She was in her 80s, had lived a wonderful life and was at peace and in heaven, he said. He proceeded to tell them that he was a pastor, and then he asked why they were there. After Janine and Steve explained what had happened, he asked if he could pray with them for Lish.

After they said a prayer, the man left to go back and see his mother.

Janine thought, "Wow, here is this man who just found out his mother died, and he wanted to offer us support."

Before the pastor walked out of the room, he told Janine, "I know your daughter will be fine."

And then, several days after Lish had arrived at the hospital, Janine met a 19-year-old girl named LeeAnn.

LeeAnn was there because her mother had been in a car accident. Her condition was compounded by her numerous health problems.

LeeAnn set up home in the right corner of the waiting room, under the only other window. She shared her story, saying she'd been caring for her mother since she was 14. Janine remembered thinking: Here's this young girl, the same age as Lish, and she was shouldering so much responsibility. She had been forced to take on the role of caregiver as a teen, and now had to make decisions about her mother's care in the hospital.

Janine's heart instantly went out to LeeAnn. They would talk, sometimes eat together, and would pray together often. Janine wanted to share with her how much God loved her and that He had great plans for her life. She didn't think anyone had ever told her how special she was.

One evening, when the other visitors left, Janine gave LeeAnn a necklace. It was a cross with the scripture, "With God All Things are Possible." Janine wanted her to have hope, the same hope she was desperately holding onto for Lish.

On another occasion, the family of a 47-year-old man sat in the far left corner of the waiting room. The unfortunate man, who was the victim of a robbery, was beaten with a cement block and left for dead. His face was unrecognizable even by his mother. The doctors requested she bring in pictures, so when they had him stabilized, they could begin putting his face back together again.

Each day we were witness to countless tales of personal tragedy and suffering.

There was the 15-year-old boy who was injured in a crash. His father had pulled into an intersection and an oncoming vehicle struck the passenger side, where the boy was sitting. Now his father sat broken hearted in the waiting room, confronted by his own guilt. Even though the accident wasn't his fault, he struggled to overcome the feeling of deep remorse over what had happened to his young son.

There was also the 18-year-old young woman who was lucky to be alive. During a horrific accident, the person driving the car she was in died upon impact. She was a beautiful young woman, very athletic and on her way to college with a full athletic scholarship. She was going to play basketball.

The 15-year-old boy and the young woman, like Lish, fell into comas.

The boy managed to wake after seven days. Not long after coming out of the coma, he was able to be placed in a chair to attempt sitting up.

The woman spent two weeks in a coma and needed a craniotomy to relieve the pressure on her brain. Like the boy, she was able to give a "thumbs-up"—a sign of consciousness—when she woke. Her father and mother were ecstatic and shared their great news with everyone.

I would've given everything I had to see Lish give a thumbs-up. As much as it shames me to say it, I wrestled with jealousy when the boy and the young woman regained consciousness, knowing that Lish was showing few real signs of being able to do the same. I just wanted so badly for her to wake.

Four times each day—at 10 A.M., 1 P.M., 5 P.M. and 8 P.M.—the families were permitted to visit their loved ones for half an hour. Four times each day, we lined up and waited for the sound of the electronic door lock. Upon hearing it, we rushed through the door and charged down the hallway like a herd of cattle. None of us wanted to waste a minute with our loved ones.

When we got to Lish, we would kiss her, talk to her and awkwardly hold her, trying not to focus on all of the equipment she was hooked up to. Sometimes I would open her eyelids just to see her eyes. Janine nicknamed her, "Sleeping Beauty." She would talk to any of the doctors and nurses who would listen, describing Lish's beautiful smile, love of life and outgoing personality. She would tell them, "Wait until you see her smile. She lights up a room."

In response, the doctors and nurses simply would force a smile. Every visit with Lish, we moved her limbs and put washcloths in her hands to relieve the strain of her clenching fists. We also talked and joked with her as if she could hear. Everybody who visited made her promises. We offered her vacations, shopping trips, pedicures and manicures, hoping the promise of something exciting would pull her from the coma.

Lish collected so many offers that her grandfather (who she affectionately referred to as her "pap") whispered to her, "I'll be your agent. If you wake up, I'll have everyone make good on their promises."

The day before her accident, Lish had her first professional manicure. Being a chronic nail-biter, she was excited with how her nails looked. Janine said Lish loved to show them off. Unfortunately, those nails proved to be a detriment in her current condition because she was now digging them into her palms. We would place a rolled wash cloth in her hand, only to come back the next visit and find it in the bed. Janine eventually managed to remove the nails, but not without sufficient frustration.

As for me, I routinely talked with Lish, whispering in her ear, "God is healing all of the broken areas. Nothing is impossible with God."

I would say: "Please wake up, Lish. You are going to come back and show them what a miracle looks like." It became a ritual to repeat those words to her at the end of each and every visit.

Another ritual we involved ourselves with was trying to arrange Lish's fist into a thumbs-up sign, hoping she would keep it that way—hoping she would respond to our care. But, every time, she instantly contracted her hand again into a tight fist.

The doctors and nurses told us Lish's movements needed to be purposeful, meaning she obeyed a command to open or close her eyes, lift a limb or attempt to speak. Things we thought were purposeful, the doctors and nurses said were not. We grew to hate the word "purposeful."

Despite our fears, we never gave up hope that God would heal Lish. Moreover, the experience had a profound impact on our relationship with God, forcing us into a deeper dependence on His grace.

My husband offered this description of the effect the accident had on him:

> "I prayed for Lish's complete and speedy recovery—body, mind and spirit. The accident deepened my prayer life so much so that I started praying every day. I got down on my knees every night. In the past, I prayed to one saint or the Blessed Mother. But when this happened, I prayed to the Blessed Mother, God the Father, Jesus, the Holy Spirit, Padre Pio, and my patron saint, James.

> "I prayed to everyone, every day and every night, hoping one would hear me and answer my prayers."

Every night now, before he climbs into bed, I still see Jim on his knees saying his prayers. He continues to pray for Lish and her recovery.

I prayed constantly, too, spending as much time as I could in the hospital's chapel.
The prayers didn't stop with us. Within days of the accident, people across the country were lifting up Lish, begging God to heal her.

We had family and friends praying. Lish was on prayer chains across the country. Everyone we spoke to would say she was on the prayer chain at their church. This gave us sincere comfort and still does.

We left nothing to chance. We blessed her with holy water from Lourdes, France, hung a rosary in her room and had the hospital chaplain give her the anointing of the sick. We also invited her Evangelical minister, Methodist and Baptist ministers, and a Roman Catholic priest to pray over her.

"God hears all prayers, regardless of what faith you are," I remember thinking.

I joked with my family that with my strong-willed mother and mother-in-law already in heaven, God must've been bombarded with their requests to make Lish well—to the point that He would be forced to oblige, saying, "All right, already."

Chapter 4

Stay Strong Alisha

As our family struggled to cope with the difficult circumstances, we were able to draw strength and encouragement from many different sources. One of the most remarkable things we encountered was the outpouring of support from Lish's friends. They launched a Facebook page called, "Stay Strong Alisha," which served to keep everyone updated on her struggles and progress. Beyond that, they all hopped on the prayer train. It was uplifting for us to see these young people show their faith and feel their support. They were people of different backgrounds and beliefs. Many of them came to visit us at the hospital and provide support. They also sent frequent emails with words of encouragement. They even brought heartfelt messages and pictures to the hospital. We posted all of the pictures in Lish's room and read each of the messages to her.

Here are just of few of the words of encouragement that provided us all with great comfort:

We are praying for your Alisha and have full confidence that God's healing will be complete in you! We love you!

Alisha I love you very much. You've been my best friend since the 7th grade. I'm just not the same without you ... You are such an inspiration to me and everyone you meet. It's so hard to be strong right now because every time I think of you I just want to breakdown and cry. There's not one day I don't think about you and all that we have been through together ... I am praying for you & I love you soooo much!

Alisha, I'm thinking about you all the time. I have been praying for you so much, and I thank God for His faithfulness to you. You are an overcomer in Christ Jesus and are more than a conqueror through Him ... I pray that you feel God's presence with you right now and that you know and believe that nothing is too difficult for Him. I love you!

We have been praying for you every day at school ... You are in our thoughts and prayers daily. We thank God for his miracle-working power and believe Him to be faithful in your life. He will ... never leave you nor forsake you ... We all love you and are rooting for you, Alisha!

Lish... Trying ever so hard to be patient as God is working His miracle in you! Wish that I could be there every day ... Missing you and your infectious smile! We love ya girl!

Alisha, We Thank God for YOU ... You've been a special Blessing—a wonderful gift of God ... You and your family are in our thoughts and prayers.

We are praying for you Alisha! STAY STRONG! Love, your cousins, Jimmy, Beth, Brianna & Marissa

Beyond simply reading her friends' messages to her, we talked constantly to Lish. Knowing that hearing is the last of the senses to go, I felt this was critically important.

All of the prayers and love and concern of others helped us avoid giving up hope, despite the grim reports from doctors and nurses. Those grim reports, in fact, gave us reason to pray even harder. We heard what the doctors were telling us, but knew our faith was stronger than their words.

Well-meaning people would stop and tell me, "Don't be mad at God." Strange as it sounds, I was never mad at God. He didn't cause this accident.

The big question I wrestled with was, "Why wasn't Lish wearing her seatbelt?" The question would creep in and out of my mind over the following months. I really felt like it was the elephant in the room; everyone thought it, but no one could ask it.

As far as we knew, she always buckled up, why not that day? It could have made all the difference in the severity of her injuries.

Chapter 5

On the Other Side of the Door

Lish looked so helpless in her coma, connected to a ventilator, feeding tube, multiple IV and antibiotic bags, a catheter, and an oxygen monitor. It crushed us to see her—so lively and outgoing only days before—now lying there so lifeless. Her arms were rigid and pulled in tight against her chest. Her legs were rigid as well, and her feet were turned inward, pushing on the bed's foot board. I would lift her eyelids to check her pupils. I found no response, no focus. Her left pupil was larger than the right, and her left eye drifted outward.

I'd seen all of this before, having worked as a registered nurse for more than 22 years. While I hadn't worked in a trauma unit, I cared for patients left fighting for their lives and saw the anguish on the faces of their family members and experienced their pain.

My dad used to say, "Get tough," though I never did. Seeing Lish connected to the equipment seemed strange, almost surreal. I felt helpless, dependent upon others to make sure the person I loved received the best possible care.

I was used to being in charge—the one in control; the one working with the doctors, giving them updates on their patients, suggesting treatment options and possible medication adjustments.

Now I found myself "on the other side of the door," and it wasn't a comfortable place to be.

Two days after the accident, a resident physician approached us in the waiting room. We gathered our chairs around him to listen to the prognosis, not knowing what to expect. Like the neurosurgeon who talked to us after the first night, this doctor said several portions of Lish's brain were bleeding, the most problematic being three areas on her brain stem, one of them resting on the area of consciousness.

"She may never wake up," he told us. He said because of severe swelling, a catheter might need to be inserted into her cranium to relieve the pressure. If that didn't work, he added, they might need to put Lish into a drug-induced coma deeper than the one she was in. And if more needed to be done, the final step would be to perform a craniotomy to relieve the pressure.

The doctor seemed certain Lish would need the craniotomy, which would involve removing a section of her skull, preserving it and replacing it later.

I left the waiting room as composed as possible and went to the bathroom to break down in private. I knew how serious all of this was but didn't want my family to know. I was sure they knew the prognosis was grim. I also knew they lacked the inside knowledge I had about the chances for Lish living a normal life even if the procedures worked.

Within a few hours of the conversation, another doctor summoned us into Lish's room. As soon as we filed in, he told Janine she needed to decide immediately on inserting the intraventricular catheter. He said increased intracranial pressure could cause a secondary brain injury and they had no time to debate the issue. He needed an answer immediately.

Not seeing any other option, Janine and Stan agreed to the procedure. We then were sent back to the waiting room to pray, cry, and hug one another so as not to completely fall apart.

Several hours after they inserted the catheter, we permitted to see Lish. Betadine (a brownish-colored topical antiseptic) stained her face and half her scalp had been shaved. She also had staples in her scalp to secure the catheter, which was connected to a monitor and a bag of 3 percent saline.

The initial reading for Lish's cranial pressure was 32 mm Hg. The normal reading for an adult is 7–15 mm Hg. I felt sick when I heard this. I wondered if too much damage had already been done and couldn't help but worry the doctors waited too long to do the procedure.

The readings fluctuated, requiring more and more saline to pull the fluid off of Lish's brain.

The reports about how well the procedure was working fluctuated, too. Told during one visit the readings were good, we would return to the waiting room elated, only to receive the opposite update during our next visit. We rode this roller coaster for weeks.

Lish was also on medication to keep her sedated. Once each day, the nurses stopped the drip to see if she responded to external stimulation. Painful stimulation forced her arm to her chest. When we saw it, we believed it to be a good sign. Then we were reminded the movement had to be purposeful. It looked purposeful to us, although the doctors and nurses assured us it wasn't.

Every instance like that—every time we had reason to hope— ended in disappointment. We wanted something to hang our hope on. We weren't asking for a rope, or even a string. All we wanted was a thread ... a tiny thread. But with each report— most of them delivered without emotion—the doctors and nurses cut that thread.

"God, please hear my prayers ... Please!" I would repeat to myself.

Every time I saw Lish, I couldn't help but tell her again and again, "God is healing all of the broken areas. Nothing is impossible with God."

Chapter 6

Knowledge—Dangerous or Helpful?

The physicians frequently took CT scans of Lish's brain. After several days in the trauma unit, she underwent an EEG to show brain activity.

At 7 A.M., Janine was summoned to the family phone in the waiting room. A female neurologist told her, "The EEG shows little brain activity."

Janine responded, "What does that mean?"

"Well, she's not brain dead," the neurologist said.

End of conversation.

The stress was beginning to take its toll on Janine. John, who had spent the night with Janine at the hospital, called my husband and me just as we arrived at the hospital. He recounted the conversation Janine had with the neurologist and said Janine was beginning to fall apart under the pressure.

I remember thinking some harsh thoughts about the doctors. I wondered to myself: Why can't these extremely intelligent and talented individuals show some empathy? They can do such marvelous things with their hands. Have they seen so much pain and suffering that they need to put up a wall between themselves and the patients and families they deal with every day? Would they be unable to function if they displayed some feelings? Had they been too sympathetic in years past that they realized it was better to remain distant and unattached?

I know that there are good and bad in all professions. Some show up to make a difference and other just show up.

I watched numerous doctors behave badly over the years. Some, I'll admit, oozed with personality and bedside manners.

Sadly, they lacked knowledge and competency. Others had all the skill in the world but lacked any semblance of personality. I realized in a trauma setting they were extremely busy and under intense pressure, but they seemed to forget there was a person—a human being—lying there helpless, and family members by that person's side feeling helpless as well.

I knew the updates had to be delivered, but did the doctors have to be so cruel in their delivery? Did they have to hit us over the head with a hammer?

Things progressed to the point where the steady stream of bad news was more than Janine could bear. I became her ears, taking the reports from the nurses and doctors and relaying them to Janine and the rest of the family. I knew from my professional experience the terminology that Lish's caregivers used to describe her condition.

I also noticed how some nurses became so attached to Lish, while a few tried to distance themselves.

I do remember several nurses tearing up while caring for Lish or giving us an update. I understood what it was like to feel for the one suffering and their loved ones. I knew from their looks how badly our Lish was struggling. Their eyes told it all.

Always one to show my emotions, I found the best thing I could do was prevent my family from seeing the heartache on my face. As a result, I shed my tears in the chapel. I prayed there for Lish to recover and for God to give us strength to cope with the situation.

About four days into Lish's coma, I started to worry about her developing "foot drop" and mentioned it to one of the nurses. I explained to the family that foot drop is caused by the weakness or paralysis of the muscles below the knee involved in lifting the front part of the foot. I was aware that with the severe injury to Lish's brain and brain stem, she was a prime candidate for this condition.

Despite what the doctors were telling us, I knew in my heart she would one day walk. When that time came, I didn't want her dragging her feet. I felt it crucial to be proactive and prevent this condition. The family agreed as well.

So, I couldn't let it go. I knew better and refused to relent until they put foot drop splints on her feet. I worked in rehab for many years and learned that preventing a problem worked better than correcting one.

A few days after they put Lish in the splints, another nurse asked why they were on. Her coworker replied, "Her grandmother is a nurse. Don't ask any more questions."

I knew a world of acronyms and abbreviations existed for almost everything: diagnoses, diseases, tests, blood work, and medication times. Those in the medical field have a language unto themselves. I tried not to let Lish's caregivers know my background, but the jargon I used gave me away. Old habits, I guess.

Still, I wanted everyone to speak to me in plain English and explain everything simply. If I had been able to think without the emotion, I probably would've been able to decipher everything without any difficulty. But we were in a trauma unit, after all, and I was in shock myself.

Beyond the foot drop issue, I noticed swelling in Lish's left arm. I mentioned it to several nurses but found my concerns summarily dismissed. The nurses said the swelling was normal, a result of an overload of fluid in her body settling in various other parts.

Again, I wasn't satisfied. I took my concerns to one of the doctors. He asked if Lish had been tested for a blood clot. I told him that, as far as I knew, she had not.

The doctor ordered an arterial Doppler test, which is a painless diagnostic tool, used to check the blood flow through an artery. During the one hour test, sound waves are bounced off the arteries, then beamed back, converted to images on a screen, and videotaped. Blood pressure readings are then taken at various locations throughout the body. A Cardiologist reviews and interprets the test.

Sure enough, they discovered a blood clot in Lish's brachial artery in her left arm. From that point on, they avoided drawing blood and inserting any IV lines into that arm. She was also put her on a blood-thinner, which she took for several months. My family was grateful I continued to ask questions.

I always told my patients that, as far as muscle tone and strength were concerned, it doesn't take long to lose what you have, but it takes a long time to get it back. I had no intentions of letting Lish simply waste away.

Even though she was in a coma, I knew passive range of motion (the movement of body parts without activating muscles) was important. Performing passive range of motion exercises with Lish would require moving different body parts through various directional motions. Someone would need to assist her, since she was unable to initiate movement on her own.

Each time we were permitted to see Lish, I asked one of the men to help with her passive leg exercises under my direction. Lish's legs were so heavy and rigid that it took considerable strength to move them. I had the men bend Lish's knees and place her foot on the bed, straighten her leg, move her ankles and make circles with her feet. It was exhausting work, but I felt it to be crucial. Throughout my nursing career, therapists would discuss with us the importance of taking a joint through its full range of motion. It preserves normal movement, they said.

I had the women move Lish's right arm and hand and left hand and fingers. The routine made family and friends feel useful and involved in her care. They all talked with her while they were doing what I considered "a labor of love."

After all, our goal from the beginning was to take Lish home to care for her. We knew we would need to get accustomed to working with her in whatever state she was discharged in.

Chapter 7

Hopes Raised ... and Dashed

One day, about a week after Lish arrived at the hospital, Jim found me in the chapel and delivered a piece of news that made me drop to my knees, praising God.

"She opened her eyes," he said.

My first thought was, "We got our miracle."

Sadly, by the time we got to see Lish during our next scheduled visit, she'd closed her eyes again.

I felt a wave of sadness like I'd never felt before. It's said that after every peak comes a valley. In a matter of an hour I had fallen from the highest peak to the deepest depth.

Twelve days into her stay, Lish's neurosurgeon visited with us a second time. He said Lish opened her eyes spontaneously for him. Like the first time, we were ecstatic. We started cheering, although it didn't last long.

"I wouldn't strike up the band," the doctor said. He then turned and left with his entourage. It would be the last time we saw him.

I remember fighting to hold back the tears until finally I was overcome by my emotions. I walked to a phone booth away from everyone and everything and began to cry.

It was probably for the best that we never saw that doctor again. If we had, I likely would've grabbed him by the collar and yelled, "Show some compassion! Can't you see our pain?"

Two weeks after the accident, on February 17, the doctors performed a tracheotomy on Lish and inserted a feeding tube into her stomach. They felt these procedures were necessary for her long-term care.

I remembered not being able to wrap my mind around the words, "long-term care." I recognized it likely meant she would be transferred to a unit for patients with little hope of recovery. I just couldn't bear thinking about Lish being in that situation.

I remember thinking things couldn't get worse. I was wrong.

The very next day, the doctors informed us Lish started to "brainstorm." None of us knew what that meant. I had never heard that term before.

The doctors also said Lish's blood pressure and heart rate escalated to nearly fatal levels.

Lish would sweat so profusely that she saturated her bedding. To combat the dangerous complications, the doctors put Lish on morphine. Sadly, this made her seem even more lifeless, leaving us to wonder how she would ever wake under such heavy sedation.

I decided to research brainstorming, which also is known as sympathetic storming. According to one website, the syndrome is sometimes seen in patients with severe brain injuries. It occurs in 15% to 33% of patients who fall into a coma.

Although brainstorming can sometimes begin within 24 hours after the injury, in many cases it does not occur until weeks after the accident. The patient often experiences a fever, high blood pressure, a rapid heart rate, and may sweat profusely and have involuntary flexion or extension of the arms or legs.

If left untreated, brainstorming can lead to secondary injury of the brain.

The research I conducted revealed that brainstorming appears to be the brain's way of "raising its level of consciousness," which sounded encouraging. This information gave us all something to hold onto—another thread to grasp—regardless of whether or not it would prove to be true.

Meantime, after two weeks of waiting for Lish to regain consciousness, we found ourselves running into reason upon reason to give up hope. The problem was we just couldn't. We loved her far too much to ever give up on her.

Chapter 8

More of the Same

Serious complications for coma patients can be life-threatening, and Lish endured her share. However, as a testament to God's grace, our girl survived each of them.

Lish battled pneumonia twice and sinus infections twice. Thankfully, aggressive antibiotic treatments knocked out the illnesses.

Her spleen, which ruptured in the accident, healed without any need for surgery. The heart contusion that she also sustained in the accident had healed with the help of medication. And, most exciting for us, the doctors were able to remove the shunt in her skull. It had been in place for 13 days.

We were all elated and encouraged, believing God heard our pleas for mercy.

The day after Lish's doctors removed the shunt, we met another physician—an apologetic third-year resident in the neurological department whom we hadn't seen before and wouldn't see again. "Sorry, I don't have any good news," he said. "She will never be the same. She will never be 100 percent. Recovery will take years if she ever wakes. She has bleeding in her brain stem which is very worrisome."

He then apologized a second time for having nothing good to say and left.

I can say one redeeming thing about the resident neurosurgeon: He tried to deliver the news in a kind manner.

Still, right or wrong, he offered no thread of hope.

He was relying only on medical knowledge. God's grace wasn't factored into the equation. Everything these doctors knew was based on MRIs, CT scans, and neurological testing. Their knowledge was all technical. None of the doctors considered the spiritual part of the equation. They never once seemed to consider that the "Great Physician" has His hand in all things.

I felt convinced none of these physicians had any experience "on the other side of the door."

At hearing the resident neurosurgeon's prognosis, Janine dropped to her knees, Jim almost passed out, and everybody else stood there speechless.

While the others eventually left the room, I lay on Lish's chest crying and begging God to prevent the prognosis from becoming the final outcome. "He can do anything," I whispered. "He can make the deaf hear, the blind see, and the lame walk. Surely he can heal our girl."

"Please, God," I sobbed. "Please heal her, please."

I then left the room for a minute to compose myself.

One of the rehabilitation doctors heard me sobbing and saw my agony. As I walked back to be with Lish, he followed. He asked what the resident in the neurology department had said. When I told him, he offered the best advice I encountered throughout the entire ordeal: "Doctors don't know," he said. "No one knows. Only God knows."

He then explained to me the importance of a coma patient's condition by the end of four weeks. For a patient who is still unconsciousness after four weeks, he or she is in either a semi-conscious state or vegetative state. Recovery from either of these could take months, or years, he said.

In a semi-conscious state, the patient is aware of his or her surroundings but can't respond fully; whereas in a vegetative state, the patient is unaware of his or her surroundings.

I stood convinced God sent this doctor to restore the thread of hope everybody else seemed to be cutting. He hadn't been assigned to our case and had no obligation to approach me.

When we parted, I thanked God for sending this doctor to deliver the message. I then walked to the waiting room, feeling better about trying to relieve the heavy burden that had fallen on our family.

Chapter 9

Our Happy Girl

What tore us apart was thinking about the Lish we knew prior to the accident. Always popular, she involved herself in school activities. She played volleyball, was on the cheerleading squad, served as secretary of the student government council, and was named prom queen her senior year. She also involved herself heavily in her church group.

Lish always smiled. It was almost impossible not to like her.

I used to tell my other seven grandchildren this riddle: "What do you have an unlimited supply of, can give one to everyone you meet, and never run out of?"

The answer: "A smile."

Lish didn't need this reminder. She was born smiling.

With her cell phone attached to her like an added appendage, she constantly sent text messages to friends.

"Why don't you just call you friends instead of texting?" I would ask.

She always offered the same reply: "Oh, grandma, we don't do things that way."

To say Lish was friendly, outgoing, and likeable would be an understatement.

As a student at the local community college, Lish worked full-time as a party hostess at Fun for All, an indoor children's playground. She loved what she did and excelled at it. Talking about how much she earned in tips on any given night always brought a smile to her face.

We hung pictures of how Lish looked before the accident above her hospital bed and on the bulletin board in her room. I knew that when a patient was hospitalized, the caregivers only saw that person in her current state. I wanted Lish's nurses and doctors to get a sense of what she looked like before—always smiling and happy.

We would tell the doctors and nurses: "If you only knew our girl before this accident. We're going to bring her back and you'll see .... She will come walking back into this unit one day."

Chapter 10

Moving Day

Lish spent 18 days connected to the ventilator since the time of her accident. When the doctors decided to let her try breathing on her own, it took four days—long and grueling for us—to wean her off the device.

Getting Lish to breathe on her own amounted to an answered prayer. The doctors had said it wouldn't be easy to wean someone off the ventilator successfully in such a short period of time. They felt it would take her much longer.

During this time, Lish opened her eyes at intervals, although they wouldn't track anything and she wouldn't blink. I would find myself thinking-where are you Lish?

At my request, a physical therapist began working with her. It was two days prior to the scheduled discharge from the trauma unit. The therapist told Janine and me that Lish opened her eyes on command during an afternoon visit with her. It was amazing news; finally a purposeful movement. But, the nurses and doctors questioned the therapist's report.

To me, however, the movement was our long awaited "purposeful" one. I trusted what the therapist had told us.

After 25 frightful days in the trauma unit, the doctors decided Lish needed to be transferred to another facility. They discussed a few options, the most prominent being a rehabilitation center or a nursing home.

We couldn't bear the thought of sending Lish to a nursing home and planned to take her home if that was the only option. She was only 19 years old, and we felt certain God had a better plan for her.

In the tri-state area, there were only two rehabilitation centers qualified to treat traumatic brain injury patients with Lish's complications. One was the brain injury unit at the now-closed UPMC (University of Pittsburg Medical Center) at South Side Hospital in Pittsburgh. The other was HealthSouth, an independent facility north of the city.

We met with nurse evaluators from both facilities. The first, Patti, a Certified Rehabilitation Registered Nurse and Rehabilitation Liaison at UPMC, insisted on reinforcing the message that Lish's injury was extremely serious and that numerous cognitive concerns existed.

"She might never get back to where she was," Patti said.

Jimmy's wife, Lora, recalled how upset she was to hear this:

> *"When Patti came into the waiting room of the trauma center, we were all sitting and waiting for our next visiting session with Lish. She was very personable and upbeat. She explained that she would go into see Lish, speak with the doctor and nurses and return with her recommendations.*
>
> *"When she came back, her body language had turned 180 degrees from before. Her tone was very solemn and her message was not very positive.*
>
> *"We were holding onto hope that Patti would find something positive to relay to us. We were so desperate for good news."*

Despite our desire for any encouraging news, Patti informed us Lish's Rancho Los Amico reading—a scale that measures cognitive ability—was a 1 or 2, with 8 being the highest.

After saying Lish "might be an angel looking down on us," Patti agreed to see if Lish might benefit from being sent to the brain injury unit for what she referred to as "coma stimulation." She explained the staff would attempt to stimulate all of Lish's senses—hearing, by speaking to her; touch, by helping her to hold items of various temperatures; vision, by us displaying family pictures as we were doing; and smell, by using fragrant body wash.

The nurse liaison from HealthSouth determined Lish wasn't stable enough to be transferred to their facility. HealthSouth didn't have a physician on-site 24 hours a day, and the nurse felt Lish needed that level of care.

We were left with the UPMC South Side Hospital as our only option, aside from the possibility of taking Lish home. We anxiously awaited word on the possibility the facility would accept her—and if the insurance company would approve the transfer.

After two days of difficult negotiations with the insurance company and many prayers, we achieved success: Lish would be moved to the UPMC South Side Hospital.

Jim, Janine, and I met Patti for a tour of the facility. Hospital officials kept the brain injury unit locked. We had to have a staff member let us in and out.

The hospital seemed pleasant and clean, and the people, friendly.

During our tour, we saw a father pushing his young son around in a wheel chair. The expressionless child had his left arm drawn to his chest and his head tilted to the side.

After saying hello to the pair, Patti turned to us and said, "This is one of our success stories. He is one year post injury."

Not one of us said a word, but our hearts dropped. All I could think was: "This can't be what our Lish will look like or be able to do after one year. Oh God, please don't let this be her."

They transferred Lish on February 27.

Lish was still relying greatly on an array of medical devices to sustain her during this time. She had the tracheostomy tube to assure a patent airway, humidified oxygen to the trach; a feeding tube for nourishment and medication; a foley catheter to drain urine from the bladder; a G-tube for draining bile from her stomach; and bilateral leg braces to keep her legs aligned properly.

All the while, the coma persisted, and her brainstorming continued at an alarming pace.

While the nurses were wonderful, they had no experience in dealing with a patient brainstorming the way Lish was. They were forced to page the on-call physician continually for instructions on medications to sedate her to prevent her blood pressure and pulse from reaching dangerous levels.

The morning after her arrival, an anesthesiologist inserted a PICC line (peripherally inserted central catheter) into Lish's right arm at the bedside for long term IV use. The anesthesiologist asked Janine and I to hold down Lish's right arm. But even in the coma, Lish possessed such tremendous strength that she kept trying to pull her arm toward her body. We held her with every bit of strength we had. Finally, the doctor succeeded. By the time the procedure was over, everybody involved was drenched in sweat.

"This is one strong girl we're dealing with," the anesthesiologist said.

After treating Lish for only four days, the doctors, nurses, physical and occupational therapists, case manager, and psychiatrist met to discuss Lish's care. They determined she needed to be sent to an acute care facility. They told Janine that Lish required more time to stabilize and that her brainstorming needed to stop before they could make any more progress with her.

The problem, as we saw it, was that Lish wouldn't receive the intensive therapy she required if her caregivers moved her to another facility. We knew how vital that therapy would be for her recovery. So, we held a meeting of our own. The decision reached from our deliberations was certain and non-negotiable—we refused to send Lish to another facility. We decided Janine would take Lish home and I would assist with the care.

We knew the job would be laborious, but weren't willing to budge. While her hospital caregivers refused to believe a miracle was in store, we knew God would bless Lish. We stood firm in our conviction that she should be home with us while that miracle unfolded.

Chapter 11

Good Morning My Child

As it turned out, the miracle we were waiting for began to unfold even before we took Lish home.

Lish had started yawning a lot shortly after arriving at the UPMC facility, and we questioned if she might be coming out of the coma.

I certainly thought our "Sleeping Beauty" might be waking up. I asked some of the medical professionals about the possibility, but they said there was no correlation between yawning and coming out of a coma.

However, on March 4, which marked one month to the day after the accident and one day after being told Lish needed to be sent to another facility, Jim and I walked into Lish's room to the greatest of surprises.

"Show your grandparents what you can do," the occupational therapist said to Lish.

To our utter amazement, she opened and closed her eyes on command, gave a thumbs-up and counted to five with her right hand. She didn't utter a word, but had a huge smile on her beautiful face.

Jim and I fell to our knees and thanked God. It was the miracle we had been praying for.

It was a glorious day!

We called everyone we knew. We couldn't wait to tell everybody who came to visit. Word spread quickly. Doctors, nurses and therapists came rushing in to see the miracle that unfolded and to rejoice with us.

The development meant Lish could stay at the brain injury unit and continue to receive the therapy she so urgently needed.

The case manager made a quick call to the insurance company and was granted 10 more days.

Janine felt terrible she wasn't there to witness Lish's awakening. Having stayed at the hospital the night before, she went home to see her other children.

Janine recounted how she first learned of the great news:

> *"I was upstairs getting myself dressed to come to the SSBI Unit, when my mom called, and she was crying. She yelled, 'Lish woke up.'*
>
> *"I wanted to know all of the details of what had just happened. My mother then proceeded to tell me that when instructed by the occupational therapist to give a thumbs-up, she did; count to five, she did; open and close her eyes on demand, she did.*
>
> *"I couldn't wait to get there and witness the miracle for myself."*

Our son Jimmy recalled that it was exactly four weeks after the accident. It was about 10 A.M. on March 4 that he received a phone call from me with the joyous news. At the time, he was in the same monthly business meeting with the same co-workers that he was with when he first learned of the accident.

This time he stepped out of the meeting when he saw my name appear on his cell phone.

The first words he heard from me were, "Lish woke up!"

Immediately, he burst back into the conference room to share the news with the group. There was clapping, cheering and tears being shed. He was getting bear hugs from all. They told him to not worry about a thing, for him to get to the hospital immediately. He had to see the miracle for himself.

Everybody experienced joy, hope, and relief beyond description that day.

While our hopes and prayers were realized, we knew how much hard work lay ahead to rehabilitate our precious girl. Getting her out of bed to a high-backed wheelchair took four nurses. She had no head control, let alone body control. She was like a big rag doll. She still had the central IV line, oxygen to her trach tube, a foley catheter, and a feeding tube. It was a lot to deal with—a floppy doll and all of her attachments.

Showering was an ordeal. Lish required a four person lift to the shower chair. They had to strap her securely in place, tilt her back and place her head in a special device to hold it in place. Then, two staff members went into the shower and did their job. They fussed over her, going so far as to shave her in the shower, apply lotions, wash and braid her hair, and apply lip gloss.

When they finished, the entire process was continued in reverse. The staff members who helped with the process walked away from the ordeal with wet, squeaky shoes, but were so delighted to be helping her.

Our family was so pleased with the care Lish received from the doctors, nurses, aides, and secretaries. She soon became one of their favorite patients.

Lish's physical therapist, Kim, turned out to be an angel from God to our eyes. She accomplished things with Lish I hadn't seen done before.

For instance, Kim got her onto a standing frame by having one therapist hold her head, having another move her feet into place, and using a sling to support her buttocks. Kim was small but unbelievably strong and determined. She even managed to get Lish—who very much looked like a wobbly rag doll—to stand up with the help of two aides and the use of some equipment.

For some reason, Lish disliked Kim. She couldn't speak at this point, but let everyone know through her actions that Kim wasn't her favorite person.

On one occasion, Lish hit Kim on the head with her elbow. And much later on in her therapy, she tried to knock her down the stairs.

Lish's behavior mortified us and made Kim sad. It wasn't like Lish to act that way. She never had a mean bone in her body.

I routinely apologized to Kim and felt certain Lish might be going through some sort of personality change. The impact from the accident injured Lish's frontal lobe. I didn't want to believe that our Lish wouldn't be the same.

Also, as it turned out, what Kim made look so easy, we later discovered for ourselves was extremely difficult.

<u>Chapter 12</u>

She's a Magician

During her time at SSBI Unit, Lish would keep pulling out her trach and feeding tubes. She would whisper the devices annoyed her. We tried to explain how crucial the equipment was for her survival, but her stubborn side eventually won.

One day during a physical therapy session, Kim and I discussed Lish's progress while we stood on opposite sides of her wheelchair. Suddenly, Lish removed the inner cannula of her trach tube. For Lish to remove this part of the trach tube, it involved turning it, lining up clips, and pulling it out. This development amazed us. The girl had turned into a magician.

As for the trach tube, the doctors gradually decreased its size over the next several weeks. This required removing one trach tube and replacing it with a slightly smaller one. The doctors hoped in time, if Lish was able to sustain breathing on her own, they would be able to remove it totally.

The speech therapist would cap it with a speaker valve during her sessions with Lish to see if she could talk.

One morning, Lish looked so very sad. The therapist asked her what was wrong. "Scared," she replied.

While Lish didn't have full insight into her situation, she did show emotion. The therapist said this was a good sign, but it broke everybody's heart to know Lish felt that way. It became difficult to leave her side, knowing how she felt.

Like a baby, she had her nights and days mixed up; staying up most of the night, and wanting to sleep all day. Between the heavy medication to prevent seizures, and her not sleeping at night, everyone struggled to have her participate in therapy.

One afternoon, she decided she wanted to return to bed. Forgetting she couldn't stand, she ended up on the floor.

Luckily, she didn't get hurt. After that incident, the doctor decided to have a sitter stay with her. Even if one of us stayed the night, the sitter remained in the room to ensure her safety.

After Lish's 18th day in rehab, her doctor felt it was safe to remove the trach tube. It marked another hurdle surpassed.

With the trach gone, Lish was left with a voice slightly above a whisper. Difficult to understand, she needed an amplifier to talk.

The speech therapist gave her a microphone headset to help her communicate more clearly. It fit on her head like a head band and had a microphone attached to it.

While the headset helped us piece together what she was saying, it annoyed Lish to the point that she decided to take it off. She did the same thing with the feeding tube and IV. It got to a point where the staff put boxing mitts on her to prevent her from removing all of her life saving equipment.

Even with a sitter or family member present, it didn't seem to stop Lish from exercising her stubborn side. On one occasion, she quietly put her hand under her sheet and grabbed hold of her stomach feeding tube. Within a few minutes, she was holding it in her hand. The sitter was amazed and embarrassed. Even the resident doctor had to laugh because the bulb within her stomach was still inflated. He said, "At least we know the bulb isn't defective because it's still intact."

By the time Lish had removed her PEG feeding tube for the third time, the doctors decided to test her ability to swallow.

The test showed she remained at a high risk for aspiration, which would put her at a greater risk for pneumonia. The doctors allowed her to only have liquids of a honey-thick consistency and finely-chopped food.

Her first meal arrived looking awful—ground-up meat and mashed potatoes with gravy dripping everywhere. Lish always loved ketchup, so I poured it on everything. It made me gag, just looking at it, though Lish made it known through her smile how wonderful it tasted.

As long as her food was doused in ketchup, Lish ate things she never touched before—even spinach, which she had never liked. The entire staff soon learned to bring ketchup every time they delivered a meal. Even the kitchen servers got to know the "ketchup girl."

Everyone fussed over Lish and always complimented the progress she was making.

And every day, a little more sunshine appeared to shine down from the heavens.

Lish was soon able to mouth, "Hi." Then, she was able to pucker her lips to blow us a kiss. And, she was even able to say, "Ma," with the use of an amplifier.

These little words and outward expressions meant more to us than one might imagine. We were filled with delight.

During the 10 weeks Lish would spend at the brain injury unit, she made steady progress. The smallest achievements made us so proud. Her ability to complete certain tasks, such as placing one cone on top of another, holding her head a little more still and following two-step commands seemed like major developments.

Not only were we elated, but so were Lish's therapists. They rejoiced in all of her accomplishments, giving us that thread of hope we so badly needed.

The therapists would set goals for Lish during their weekly staff meetings, which they held on Tuesdays. By Thursday, Lish had met most of the goals.

Everyone on the unit started to refer to her as the "Miracle Girl." They enjoyed watching her progress and were amazed with how quickly she continued to improve.

Lish had started off in a high-back chair, supported with pads, a safety belt, and a lapboard on which she could rest her constantly moving arms. After several weeks, the therapists reduced the amount of support she required to sit in her wheelchair.

Lish's doctors decided to try serial casting on Lish's lower left leg to decrease the contracture (tightening of the muscle) that was developing. The process involved applying and removing a lightweight cast weekly. The angle of the cast is gradually changed to slightly stretch the muscles and to move the joint a little closer to the correct position.

Every Monday, Kim replaced the cast, which wasn't an easy task. Plaster flew everywhere with Lish moving about wildly. Anyone who walked within range got splattered with the stuff, including Janine, who was there to assist in the process.

Lish wore a foot-drop splint on her right foot and bilateral wrist splints on her hands and forearms to keep them in proper alignment. Every now and again, she would wiggle her way out of the foot-drop splint, and the wrist splints as well. We found ourselves constantly reapplying them and repositioning Lish in her chair or in her bed.

One day, a nurse approached Janine to share something she had recalled. She explained that she was on duty the day Lish arrived at the facility. The nurse recalled how the attending doctor told her to "hope for the best but expect the worst."

I can't put into words how frustrated and sad all of this pessimism made me. I said it before and I'll say it again: Evidently, these doctors put no stock in our "Great Physician."

Chapter 13

A Visit with Her Siblings

About six weeks after the accident, Janine decided she felt comfortable having Lish's sister and brothers pay her a visit.

Trying to prepare them for what they would encounter, Janine spent a lot of time explaining what had happened and how badly Lish was hurt.

The kids asked tons of questions:

"Will she look the same, mommy?"

"Why does she have to stay in the hospital for such a long time?"

"When is she coming home?"

It was a Sunday afternoon when Janine took the children (Alexis, 10; Steven, 8; and Anthony, 4) to the hospital. I immediately could tell by the look in their eyes how frightened they were.

"The tubes looked creepy and the monitors scared me," Alexis told me later in private.

She commented that although Lish looked the same, she didn't act the same. It wasn't the sister Alexis knew before the accident.

I remember Lish fidgeting in the wheelchair so much that day. Her legs kept falling off the footplates, her arms kept falling off the lapboard, and her head bobbed all over the place. It seemed like a continual effort to readjust her and pull her back into the seat of the chair.

Shortly after her siblings came to visit, Lish's cousins—Brooke, Brian, and Matt—stopped in with Jimmy and Lora.

I could sense they were terrified as well.

Brooke started to cry. Being 13, she understood more fully what was going on. The younger ones just stood their distance. It was as though Lish was contagious.

But, one by one, they slowly got a little closer. One touched her hand and another touched her arm. Then they began trying to talk with her a little.

At one point, we took Lish to a small park across the street, giving the children a chance to run and play together as usual. Everything seemed normal again, until we looked at Lish.

As I noted, Lish continued to struggle with holding her head up. She also had trouble using her right hand and needed total assistance eating, bathing, dressing and grooming. And, she continued to be incontinent of both bowel and bladder.

This lasted for 10 months after the accident and proved to be difficult for some to deal with.

It's one thing to change a baby. It's an entirely different thing to change an adult. While it had little effect on me, it was hard on Janine and Lish's other caregivers.

Beyond that, it took months before the doctors cleared Lish to drink thin liquids. Each time they tested her ability to swallow, we hoped for positive results, only to find out she continued to run the risk of aspirating if she drank something like water or Coke. Everything we gave her to drink required the addition of several teaspoons of a thickening agent.

Though Lish was making progress, there was still a long way to go.

Chapter 14

Easter

On Easter Sunday, our entire family gathered in a conference room to spend the day with Lish. Everyone brought food, which included Lish's favorites: ribs and a strawberry and cream Frappuchino from Starbucks.

John's fiancée, Monica, made the ribs and pureed them. We spoon-fed them to Lish, and after adding a healthy dose of thickener to the frapp, fed that to her as well.

We tried to make the day as normal as possible. Sadly, it just wasn't.

Lish was so tired and exhausted that at one point she put her head down right into her food. Moreover, she slid partially out of her wheelchair a couple of times, forcing us to constantly prop her back up.

Lish's siblings and cousins tried to watch a movie but couldn't keep from being distracted by the confusion caused by all of the attention that Lish required.

We all wore brave faces, but our hearts ached for the Lish of old—the life of the party, the smiling, happy girl.

Even though she was making progress, we couldn't help but wonder if she would plateau the way patients often do—the way the doctors said she would.

I continued to pray harder than I ever had in my life. But, I found myself casting burdens on God and then taking them back again. My anxiety grew. I knew I needed to get out of the way and let God handle everything.

To use a popular cliché, I needed to "let go and let God."

"Not my will, but Thine be done," I would repeat to myself.

My great fear was that it might not be God's will to return Lish to being a whole, intact, functioning human being.

When that worry would creep into my mind, I would remind myself of some words of encouragement a dear friend shared with me, and which I passed on to my family: "Hope in the face of hopelessness. Believe in the face of despair. Love like there is no tomorrow."

Chapter 15

Going Home

The time came to take Lish home—largely because the insurance company refused to pay for additional inpatient care. Lish's doctors and therapists set the discharge date for May 8.

Looking back, I recall how uncertain we were about what the future had in store for us. In my mind, this might have been a good thing. Had any of us known the difficult road that lay ahead, we might have hesitated for a minute, and wondered if we could do it.

To prepare us for Lish's ongoing care, her therapists asked everyone who would be directly involved to meet at the hospital for instructions. The group included Jim and me, Lish's parents, and her two aunts and uncles.

The therapists spent time with each of us, running demonstrations and answering questions. We were shown the proper techniques for how to transfer her into and out of a wheelchair, and how to walk with her using a walker. The men were shown how to get her up and down stairs.

One week before discharge, we took Lish to her home in Baden for a day. We did this for a few reasons: to gauge what adaptations would be required at home, to see if we were able to care for all of her needs, and to understand what further assistance or instructions we might need before discharge.

At this point in her recovery, Lish was able to control her head, sit in a standard wheelchair with a lap belt to keep her secure, and transfer into her wheelchair with moderate assistance. Any transfer involved Lish doing half the work and a caregiver doing the other half. Lish would turn in bed, then bridge and lift—a rehab technique I showed everyone early on. The process involved having Lish bend her knees, plant her feet on the bed and raise her buttocks so she could move to another surface.

I used this technique on daily basis in my nursing days. It helps get the patient on the bedpan, dress and undress, and move in bed. I never thought I'd use it to help my granddaughter perform those tasks.

As for the trial day at home, to say that it proved to be challenging would be a bit of an understatement.

The work we previously did with Lish at the hospital seemed entirely different in the house. We soon realized several obstacles ...

- The hallways were too narrow for a wheelchair.

- The door to the powder room on the first floor wasn't wide enough for a walker.

- The chairs at the kitchen table didn't slide far enough in (making it impossible for Lish to reach the table).

- The stairway had only one rail, which wasn't strong enough to support Lish's weight and that of the person assisting her. We feared the force would pull the rail right off the wall.

- The family room furniture sat lower than Lish had grown accustomed to. Lowering herself down with the little strength she had resulted in what we referred to as a "plop."

- Helping Lish get back up after she sat down on the family room furniture required much assistance and instruction.

At the conclusion of the day, we returned Lish to the brain injury unit. On the way to the facility, we made a list of all the adaptations that would be needed to make the home safe and accessible for her: Jim decided to install rails in all of the bathrooms. Her other grandfather would arrange to have double railings installed in the stairwell. We decided to buy special eating utensils and a plate with a lip to assist in her feeding herself. And, we agreed to get sliders for the kitchen table and the chair Lish would use.

As we were wheeling Lish back to her hospital room, the staff was anxiously asking us how everything went. I'm not certain, but I think they knew by the way we looked, that it had been a very rough day.

After dropping Lish off, and feeling totally exhausted, the reality of how difficult it was going to be to care for her 24/7 hit us all.

Still, we had no reservations about caring for Lish at home.

UPMC fought with the insurance company for as long as they could. The carrier terminated her care at the facility.

The option of sending Lish to a nursing home still existed in the minds of her doctors and therapists. But it wasn't an option for us. We all agreed that we weren't putting our 19-year-old girl in a facility where she wouldn't receive the therapy and love she needed.

My heart ached for Janine. Not only did she have to care for her other children, ages 4, 6 and 10, but now she was required to spend most of her time caring for Lish, who needed the attention an infant demands.

At 5 feet 8 inches, caring for Lish made caring for a newborn look easy.

When the big day arrived, the staff at SSBI Unit gathered around Lish to say goodbye, piling on hugs and kisses and requesting she come back to visit.

It was Janine and I who took Lish home. It was somewhat frightening to pull away from the facility, knowing we were on our own now. Even with my experience in nursing, I had never cared for a patient 24 hours a day and 7 days a week. I felt that both the physical and emotional stress was going to be difficult.

On her discharge day, Lish remained incontinent of bowel and bladder. She still needed nearly total care when it came to feeding, dressing and bathing. She was beginning to help in those areas, but had a long way to go.

On the day before her discharge date, she had developed severe hand and leg tremors, making every activity that much more difficult for her.

During meals, someone had to help Lish scoop her food onto a weighted utensil and guide it to her mouth. She drank from a two-handled cup with guidance.

It took two of us and constant cuing to transfer Lish from her wheelchair to her walker.

Once she got behind the walker, it took two of us to help her stay balanced. We needed to support the full weight of her body and advance the walker at the same time. It was the only way to keep her upright.

Strangely, every time she passed a mirror, she stopped, looked at herself, and said, "I look so pretty." It didn't matter if she had a shower cap on and a bath towel wrapped around her. Every mirror produced the same surprised remark.

We tried to train her on the toilet the way you would a child. We made frequent trips with her to the bathroom and started limiting how much she drank three hours before she went to bed.

We even set up a hospital bed in the dining room with layers of padding, but we struggled to get her from there to the bathroom. It's a tiny bathroom to begin with, and fitting Lish and two helpers amounted to quite the task.

Each time before Lish rested, we had to go through the process of getting her to the toilet and then back into the bed. We were attempting to toilet train our girl.

When Lish napped, we all napped. When she would wake an hour to an hour-and-a-half later, we found not only her drenched, but her linens as well. We had to wash her and change her and the bed linens every time.

Unlike hospital beds, Lish's bed at home didn't raise up and lower back down. The constant bending over took its toll on our backs.

Our techniques didn't work 100 percent of the time. We wound up continuously washing Lish's bedding and clothing.

And that's not to mention having to bathe Lish constantly to protect her skin from breaking down.

After the accident, yogurt became one of her favorite foods. Prior to the accident, she couldn't stand yogurt. Whenever we took her to the doctors or to therapy, she would say, "do you have any yogurt?"

If we didn't want to use the thickener, we could give Lish honey-thick liquids from a special cup, designed to prevent any fluid from getting into her lungs. It had two handles for her to try and hold onto.

The large bib we draped around her somehow didn't protect her clothing. For that matter, it didn't protect her hair or the floor. After each meal, she and the room needed a healthy cleaning.

Lish's progress moved quite slowly. She continued to be extremely tired, wanting to sleep most of the day. If she was placed on a cot to do exercises, she would grab for a pillow and fall asleep. The family's job was to be constant cheerleaders and push Lish to do what the therapist expected her to do, while keeping her awake long enough to complete the task at hand.

Beyond the physical difficulties, she seemed to be going through a personality change. She would say hurtful and nasty things to her mother, such as "I hate you" and "You're stupid." Janine would cry to me and asked the doctor what she should do. The physician said to tell her as you would a child, "That is not appropriate talk." She also said to reinforce that it was the injury talking not Lish.

Everyone struggled to push forward, doing the best they could.

<u>Chapter 16</u>

Cursing Jag

At 6 A.M. on May 10, Janine called.

"Alisha is saying, 'Fuck, damn, shit, ass,' over and over again," she said. "I can't get her to stop."

I told Janine to call 911 and that her dad and I would be out as soon as possible.

When we arrived at Janine's home within an hour of her phone call, we found an ambulance crew attending to Lish.

Lish was expressionless when we saw her, although the obscenities flowed like water. Nothing any of us could do interrupted her ranting.

I held Lish's head between my hands and saw nothing in her eyes. There was no expression on her face. This freighted me tremendously.

I rode with Lish in the back of the ambulance and Janine rode in the front. Just as we pulled in front of the emergency room entrance at the hospital, Lish stopped cursing.

The episode lasted exactly 2 hours—a very, very long 2 hours.

Once again, the doctors drew blood and conducted a CT scan. Like before, the results showed nothing unusual. The doctors were unable to provide an explanation for Lish's episode.

Lish's physicians decided to increase the anticonvulsant medication she was taking from 1500 mg to 2500 mg. One side effect of that medication was fatigue. We had been battling to keep Lish awake, and this increase in medication only made it harder for her to keep her eyes open.

Chapter 17

Outpatient Therapy

Janine didn't want any time to elapse between inpatient and outpatient therapy. We agreed as a family how important therapy was for Lish's recovery. So, Lish started her outpatient therapy on May 12 at the UPMC facility on Pittsburgh's South Side—several blocks from the inpatient department she had just been discharged from.

After getting Janine's other children up and off to school, Janine, Lish, and I made the two-hour roundtrip, three days each week, to the outpatient department.

Lish had to endure three hours of therapy during each visit. This consisted of physical, occupational, and speech therapy, which were conducted one right after the other.

After a five-hour day, which included the commute, we were exhausted. However, the day was far from over. Janine's younger children would be arriving home from school, which meant meals had to be prepared for that hungry group in addition to taking care of laundry and homework and baths.

With Lish making slow progress during this period, we sometimes grew frustrated and couldn't help but wonder what the future held for her.

The outpatient physical therapists weren't able to walk Lish as successfully as Kim had done at the hospital. Lish needed constant cuing to fully participate. All she really wanted to do was sleep. Anytime the therapists placed her on a mat, she found a way to lie down. The anticonvulsant medication kept her fatigued, which created a struggle for everyone, including her therapists.

We labored to keep up with taking Lish to therapy so frequently and caring for her and the other children at home. We thought about asking the doctor to prescribe home care for

Lish. It would have made life much easier. But in the end, we decided it was in her best interest to go to outpatient therapy where they had the equipment that might eventually get her walking again.

On several occasions, the therapists did put her into a harness device and manually moved her feet. One therapist helped with her upper body and another assisted in moving her feet.

Because of her tremors, Lish struggled with other tasks such as trying to place clips on a rod during occupational therapy. The clips frequently snapped and went flying. She would say, "Those darn tremors."

This therapy routine was maintained and followed for four long and grueling weeks.

On May 15, Lish had an appointment with her physical rehabilitation physician, who said she was pleased with the progress Lish was making and felt she would continue to improve. These were the words of encouragement we desperately needed to hear.

Janine and I explained how violent Lish's tremors had become. On the way to the office that day, Lish literally shook the car while we were stopped at a red light. I know it is difficult to believe, but I was in the back seat and I couldn't understand how anyone could have such violent tremors.

The doctor referred us to a motion specialist, Dr. Burton.

I hadn't heard of a neurologist who specialized in that area, but was anxious for Lish to see him. I hoped he could treat the tremors, knowing how they affected her everyday activities.

The tremors were so bad that it was impossible for Lish to hold a cup without splashing its contents everywhere. When she tried to feed herself, she wound up with food all over her face. Her legs shook so badly it was difficult to keep them on the wheelchair footplates.

Luckily, we were able to get an appointment with Dr. Burton rather quickly. He turned out to be a pleasant man with a Scottish accent. After examining Lish, he told us that he could prescribe medicines to help control the tremors.

"The problem," he said, "is the medications all have side effects—fatigue and memory loss among the most common."

He suggested holding off on adding any new medicines, saying he felt it was best to wait and see if the tremors lessened on their own. This later proved to be a very wise decision.

Chapter 18

Stages of Recovery

We were truly blessed, that although Lish went through many phases of recovery, most of the unpleasant ones were short lived.

The inhibition and inappropriate behavior was a very difficult concept for Lish and us to understand and to deal with.

Because one of the injuries affected her frontal lobe, the "filter" between what Lish thought and what she said was almost nonexistent.

For instance, you might see someone in an ugly dress and not say a word. Not Lish. If she thought it, she spoke it, which proved quite embarrassing at times.

One evening, she phoned a boy she had dated a few times. I heard her say, "I want to have six to nine children with my husband." It was quite a conversation.

I had an extremely difficult time trying to explain to Lish why that statement wasn't appropriate. After I had shared my thoughts, Lish called several of her girlfriends to hear what they thought about her comments. She wanted, and needed, her peers to validate her remarks. Fortunately, they reinforced what I was telling her.

Then there was the time she felt she needed to "save" one of her therapists. During one of her therapy sessions, Lish was using an auto-ambulator (a device designed to get people walking again by supporting their body with a harness and moving their legs on a treadmill with the help of robotic limbs) when she decided the therapist needed to become a Christian. She insisted he repeat the salvation prayer after her.

I could tell how uncomfortable the therapist was. I was uncomfortable, too. But my attempts to get Lish to stop didn't work.

When that very long hour was over, Lish and I had an extended talk about it not being appropriate. I tried to explain that everybody has their own religious beliefs and that therapy wasn't the time or place to try converting that man.

I reinforced the message that her most pressing need was to heal and work on getting back to being independent. I told her then she could tell her story and spread her beliefs in a more appropriate manner when the time was right.

Incidents like these reoccurred often over the first year. None of us were ever prepared to handle them. We didn't know how to handle them. We felt at times like we were dealing with a child in an adult's body.

When a child says inappropriate things, people laugh or consider them cute. That's not the case with a 19-year-old young woman.

During the months it took for Lish to regain bowel and bladder control, there were many moments of frustration and even a few disagreements.

Those of us caring for her tried to get her to the bathroom every two hours and not give her liquids after 8 P.M. Even so, she and the bed linens would be soaked in the morning.

We tried using two diapers and four pads, but these attempts proved futile.

One afternoon between therapy sessions, Lish and I were eating lunch in the cafeteria. She had refused to go to the bathroom prior to sitting down, denying the need to go. I had just cut her food and sat down, when she said, "I have to go to the bathroom."

Her next words were, "It's too late."

When I questioned why she didn't tell me sooner or try to hold it, she said, "I told you."

I felt like I was dealing with a child.

Lish needed constant reminders to hold her stomach in. Her therapists stressed how it would help with her balance.

When I would remind her, she'd get upset and say adamantly, "I am holding my stomach in."

Several of us in the family tried to reason with her, telling her we wouldn't bring it up if she was doing it. It took several months to finally sink in.

Now she says, "I see what you mean."

So many times throughout the first year, Lish would say how sorry she was for putting us through this ordeal. She would cry and even say she should have stayed in heaven.

About a week after being discharged from SSBI Unit, our entire family—including aunts, uncles, and cousins—were with Lish at Janine's home. Lish totally stunned us all when she whispered, "I saw Jesus."

Her voice was still so very low and her speech difficult to understand. We had her repeat what she had just said. She responded: "I saw Jesus when I went to heaven. He had shoulder length hair and the most beautiful eyes. He told me to go back down. I then said, 'To Hell, Jesus?' And he said, 'No, Lish, you have work to do.'"

Everyone who was present was astonished. We all looked at one another in disbelief. Could what she was saying be true? Did she really see Jesus? Every time she repeated this story, every detail was exactly the same. Our doubts turned into belief. We all knew Jesus had a big hand in this journey.

I would tell Lish that God is bringing her and the family through this for a purpose. I told her, "I believe the purpose is to spread hope when there is no hope, belief where there is doubt, and encouragement in the face of tragedy."

I can't tell you how much Lish wanted to return to the routines and social life she loved prior to that awful, life-changing day of the accident.

As I have said before, Lish was always so outgoing and talkative. Thank God her personality was basically the same. None the less, she longed to be able to walk like before, use her hands without tremors, get back to work and school and spend time with her friends.

The tears would flow when she focused too long on these things, and all we could do as a family was hold her and cry along with her.

Every day we had to orient Lish to time, date, and place. When we would say, "It's Monday, May whatever," she would respond, "I'm 19. Holy crap!"

We would laugh and tell her she was still so young. But the concept didn't sit well. In her mind, she was "so old."

Lish didn't recall her birthday, which was February 3, the day prior to the accident. Nor did she recall her birthday party, which was a few days earlier—the day the Steelers won the Super Bowl.

She frequently asked if she was being punished or if it was all a bad dream.

My heart broke for Lish one day during occupational therapy. Her task was to peel a cucumber and cut it up. Because of her tremors, it took 50 minutes.

Part of me wanted to cry, but the other part was so very proud. Lish never stopped once or said she couldn't do it.

Those darn tremors affected so many things she did. Holding a cup in her hand often resulted in a shower of water going everywhere. Her handwriting was so shaky and all over the paper. Feeding herself took such a long time as she tried to navigate the utensil to her mouth, but we knew we couldn't do it for her. Just like a baby, how will they ever learn if we do everything for them?

During her periods of frustration, we as a family found ourselves asking, "What would the future hold for our Lish?"

The truth is, during difficult times, all anyone can see is the pain and the darkness. This is when we lose sight of God. I admit to being guilty of this, giving my worries and concerns to God and then taking them back.

The purest prayer is one that makes our will yield to God's.

I have become much better at "letting go and letting God" and trusting that God will do what is necessary. There is such a feeling of relief when God carries our burdens. With every part of my being, I truly believed God could heal our girl, the hard part was wondering when it would happen.

Lish was fortunate the doctors started her on an antidepressant early in her treatment. We truly believed it kept her from sinking into a severe depression. Sure, she had her ups and downs, but she was quickly able to return to a more normal plane.

Chapter 19

Kinesio Taping

On June 10, Jim and I took Janine and her four children to our home in Kissimmee, Florida.

Janine had done a lot of research on the computer finding a facility that specialized in treating patients with a brain injury. It ended up that we enrolled Lish in an outpatient program at Celebration Hospital Florida.

Lish immediately grew to love each of her therapists there, giving them all nicknames: Juicy Jamie, the occupational therapist; Brilliant Brunella, the physical therapist; and Cool Christina, the speech therapist.

Jamie and Brunella had recently finished a class in Kinesio Taping, a technique developed by the Chinese. They noted when Lish tightened her core muscles, her leg tremors ceased. They agreed it was worth trying the tape to increase her core muscle strength and as a side effect, control her tremors.

They applied the tape to her abdomen and buttocks in a distinctive manner, telling us to keep it on for four to five days.

Whenever Lish relaxed her core muscles, she would feel the tape. At that point, a message would shoot to her brain to contract those muscles. The technique worked wonders.

We couldn't help but wonder if something as simple as Kinesio tape could replace medications.

The therapists used the tape over several months, and the tremors decreased steadily. What a blessing this was-no more medication to add to her fatigue.

Chapter 20

Magical Place

When Lish was a little girl, she and her pap would watch the movie *Beauty and the Beast* over and over and over again. It was definitely her favorite Disney movie. She loved the character Bell and would pretend to be her. She knew the words by heart and would repeat them just as Bell did in the movie.

Our family's first visit to Disney World with Lish was amazing. She was just a little girl at the time, but was already one of the most outgoing and friendly children you could imagine, almost to a fault. She would approach strangers in stores and smile and talk with them. It actually concerned us at times. Most people were so warm and friendly, but there were a few who gave us looks.

No matter how many vacations we went on, our favorite was still the Magic Kingdom at Walt Disney World. It held such wonderful memories for us.

Now we were in Florida with Lish, who was 19 and recovering from a traumatic brain injury. The road was slow, but she was definitely moving in the right direction.

One never knows what each new day will bring. Sometimes life seems full of amazing coincidences—or perhaps they are more than just coincidences. I can recall one occasion in particular when we experienced one of life's "amazing coincidences."

One day, Janine, Lish, and I went to a cosmetic store to buy some eye shadow and to hopefully learn the correct technique to apply it. We knew John and Monica's wedding was coming soon and wanted to be prepared for the big day. That was where we met a beautiful young woman working at the cosmetic counter. She started talking with Lish in such a sweet manner and applying the eye shadow. The two of them talked about how much they liked Florida. Lish shared with her that she dreamed of doing an Internship at Disney one day. When

Jane, the girl at the counter, said she worked at Disney, Lish's eyes lit up.

She asked Jane, "What do you do?"

Jane wasn't permitted to say.

How sad Lish looked.

Jane then said, "All I can say is, I call my father, 'Papa.'"

Lish yelled, "You're Bell!"

They hugged and laughed and talked like old friends. Lish told her that was her favorite Disney character. It was so good to see Lish interacting as she had done prior to the accident. She was so friendly, engaging, and lively.

Jane then said she wanted us to be her guests at Disney World. We turned into children, so excited and happy. We exchanged e-mails and phone numbers and told her we would be in touch after the wedding.

Chapter 21

John and Monica's Wedding

Jim and I weren't sure if our son John would ever meet the right girl. By the time he reached his early thirties, he'd dated a lot of very nice women, although none proved to be "the one."

His physical appearance and demeanor reminded Jim and me of his maternal grandfather—tall with dark brown hair and piercing blue eyes.

John is quiet, and his thoughts and feelings run deep. I would tell him, "Still waters run deep."

When he met Monica, things seemed to click right away. He felt, after dating for one year, it was time to get engaged.

I was so thrilled when he asked me to go with him to look for an engagement ring. After visiting several jewelry stores, he chose a ring very much like the one his dad gave me almost 43 years ago—a beautiful solitaire diamond in a white gold band.

John was very excited getting ready for the big night. After spending a long time showering, grooming and dressing, he immerged looking so handsome. After placing the ring securely in his pocket, I kissed him goodbye and Jim gave him a hug. Off he went with a big smile on his face.

John and Monica had a favorite restaurant they enjoyed going to—a small, cozy eatery that overlooked the city. It was a cold November evening in 2008 when they went there for a very special dinner. It was there that John popped the question.

Shortly after the proposal, we received a phone call. Both he and Monica couldn't wait to share their exciting news. "We're engaged," she said. Jim and I were so happy to be a part of this wonderful time in their lives.

John and Monica chose July 11, 2009 for their wedding date. I was thrilled that most members of our family were asked to participate in the wedding ceremony.

John's oldest brother, Jimmy, was to be the best man. And Jimmy's children also were given roles: His daughter, Brooke, was to be a junior bridesmaid, and his son, Brian, a reader.

Janine and Lish were chosen as bridesmaids, and Janine's younger daughter, Alexis, a flower girl.

Steve, Janine's husband, was picked to be one of the ushers.

Several months after John had proposed to Monica, the accident happened and everyone's joy over the wedding was dashed.

The first time John and Monica came to the trauma center to see Lish, they said they were going to postpone the wedding. They weren't able to envision a happy occasion in the face of such tragedy.

Jim, Janine, and I emphatically said no. We truly felt life must go on. That included the wedding.

We told them everyone, including Lish, would be there.

Lish would be a bridesmaid as planned, we said.

I can recall dreaming one night that we had to carry Lish into church on a stretcher—still connected to the life support system, with tubes coming from every orifice—because she remained comatose, as the doctors predicted. I woke up and prayed, "Please God, help her."

Jim and I had long hoped for the day when John would marry like his brother and sister. Because of the accident, we couldn't even think about it now or devote any time to the planning. We had five months until the wedding and felt a lot could happen in that time.

Planning a wedding is trying at best. Then you add a family emergency on top of everything and the load gets unbearable at times.

Monica put it this way ...

> *"I'm a very organized person who likes to get things done right away. Shortly after John proposed, I was out shopping for my gown, arranging for the church and receptions hall, thinking of the attendants and getting everything done as early as I could.*
>
> *"John is much more laid back, and let me do my thing.*
>
> *"John and I thought it best if we postponed the wedding. But his mom said, 'Life must go on; the wedding goes on as planned.' She said Lish would be there one way or another even if they had to bring her in on a stretcher."*

Monica also explained how lucky she was to have her mother there to help:

> *"She and I have always been extremely close. We are best friends. She loves John and was so happy that we were getting married. She was my rock. We did all of the shopping, made the arrangements and talked for hours about all of the plans. This provided a happy place for my mind to go."*

Over the next several months, our hopes and expectations about Lish's future were uncertain. The unknown was difficult, never knowing if she would stop at a particular stage or continue making progress. When we arrived at the SSBI Unit and she wasn't able to hold her head up, we envisioned her at the wedding in that condition.

But, as the months progressed, and so did Lish, we could envision her at the wedding being wheeled around in a wheelchair with a strap around her waist for safety.

Monica's bridal shower took place May 17—eleven days after Lish was discharged from the rehabilitation facility. It marked the first time some family and friends had seen Lish in a while. They all remarked about how great she looked and how well she was doing. Janine and I weren't so sure. Every time we looked at her, she had her head down, dozing.

Considering it was three and a half months after the accident, it seemed remarkable she was able to do as much as she did. Just being there was a huge accomplishment.

At the same time, physical challenges persisted. Lish wasn't able to use her right arm or leg well. The incontinence continued and her speech was so low it was difficult for others to understand her. She failed to pass three swallow tests, so she was still drinking honey-thick liquids.

The night after the shower, Janine and I slept a little better because we knew Lish could attend the wedding in a wheelchair and not on a stretcher, in a coma attached to life-support equipment.

I figured she may sleep throughout the ceremony, but she would be there.

"Thank you Jesus," I said.

The wedding took place as planned. The weatherman forecasted strong winds and severe thunderstorms. Normally, I would have fretted.

To be honest, I would have fretted about everything. But my attitude changed. It became, "WHATEVER!"

Grace, a longtime dear friend of Lish's, offered to do her hair and makeup for the big day. She did wonders covering over the short spikes of hair that were beginning to grow again on her scalp. She accomplished this with a lot of talent and an artificial hair piece.

Grace later wrote a very moving and heartfelt paper that she shared with us.

It read as follows:

I first met Alisha Danielle Webb-Camp when I was turning 8 years old. We both attended a girls-only, lock-in style sleep over at our local church. My family had recently moved to the area which had devastated my social life. I was struggling to get back on my feet. All of the girls at the lock in had their own clique to lay their sleeping bags next to. I wandered around the class room we were set up in, feeling nervous and out of place when a beautiful, bubbly girl with mocha skin approached me and introduced herself as Ally. From that moment on I seamlessly fused with Ally's clique because of her confidence and outgoing personality that led her to introduce herself to the new girl.

This is a prime example of Alisha's character and charisma in action. She has always put effort into making everyone in a group or at a get-together feel comfortable and important. She loves to be the center of attention as long as it helps someone else to feel accepted. Through the years those qualities have not faded. Alisha has coined countless phrases and invented exclamations that are now used in every day conversation between friends, as well as created accents from unknown places. Her obsession with other cultures is not only infectious, but it has caused our group of friends to be full of diverse ethnicities.

When someone has had such a positive influence on your life it is impossible to imagine something negative happening to them. February 4, 2009, turned that impossibility into reality. I was 19 and in cosmetology school full-time. I had off the first Wednesday of each month and was in the middle of homework at my boyfriend's house when I got the text: "Pray for Lish, she was in a car accident, she's in the ICU at Allegheny General." I immediately dialed Alisha's best friends from our church and we decided to visit her that evening. No one had any further details about the accident or what condition Alisha was in at the time. We met at a small store off of the interstate to pick up flowers and snacks for her family and then set off to the hospital, speculating without really letting ourselves think of the grim possibilities.

Even as we found our way through the hospital and to the Intensive Care Unit on the fourth floor, I still had not let the news sink in. I was surrounded by off-white walls and tile floors and medical personnel, but had not yet realized that my best friend was a patient only a few rooms away from the elevator I was exiting. My girl friends and I did not link arms or hold hands; we were all in our own worlds. We approached the ICU doors.

When we first entered the waiting room for family we saw Alisha's mother, Janine. It took her a moment to realize that we knew each other. For the next few weeks her red rimmed eyes were perpetually filled with tears threatening to spill over and her voice shook with every word. I don't remember what sympathies were exchanged or who else was there. I only remember the face of a devastated mother and hugging her with sincerity. It happened to be visiting hours when our group arrived and we were allowed to see Alisha for the first time.

Walking down the hall to Alisha's room with her family and our friends was surreal. We kept close together and didn't touch a thing. We passed sterile environments and other ICU patients hooked up to monitors on inclined hospital beds. We rounded the nurse's station and went straight into Alisha's room. There in front of me lay my best friend, unconscious, surrounded by machines that attached to tubes and wires leading into her head, torso, and arms. I had somehow expected her to be awake, which was delusional. I was shocked and speechless at the sight before me; the only thing I could do was cry.

I am still speechless when asked about how it felt to see Alisha laying in the hospital. God gave us emotions to describe the things we cannot say. Sometimes there are no words to express the way something makes us feel.

I was later informed of the details surrounding the accident, as well as the trauma Alisha's body was suffering. The most amazing part of seeing Alisha that day was the complete absence of bruising or facial trauma. So much had happened to her brain within her skull, but there was no evidence on the outside. Despite how good she looked, the reality of what had happened began to sink in. Questions begged to be answered. When will Alisha wake up? Will she be herself? Will she wake up at all? No one had any answers. But everyone had hope.

The following weeks are still a blur to me. I know I visited Alisha after school every day that I wasn't working. I remember talking to her, touching her arms and legs, and trying to project positivity. I tried not to cry in front of her. Her grandmother printed out the cards and well wishes that her friends who could *not visit would send and I'd read them out loud to her. We would pray for her and tell her to wake up. Then at the end of visiting time everyone would leave the room so Janine could say goodnight to her daughter.*

In March, when Alisha finally awoke from her coma, her grandma let me know. I could have screamed, I was so excited. Although the road to recovery is long, Alisha has kicked the grim reports from the doctors out the door. She has taken something that could have been so negative and made the choice to be positive and enjoy life. Even in the darkest situation there is always light.

The weather on the morning of the wedding was lousy—cloudy, overcast, and rainy. However, by the time we arrived at the church, the sun was out and the sky was blue.

Janine pushed Lish down the aisle in her wheelchair and entered the pew beside her. She was nervous that Lish may say or do something inappropriate. But that never happened. They both looked more gorgeous than they ever had before.

Lish held her bouquet a little lopsided and wore that famous smile to complete the look.

Our family pastor had agreed to travel to Monica's church and perform the ceremony. It was beautiful. He told some funny stories and personal tidbits about Monica and John. The guests laughed and the mood was light.

It meant so much having family and friends celebrate such a happy occasion. They were all with us on our difficult journey and now we all had reason to rejoice.

At the reception, Lish's partner Donny was so kind. He stood her up, and with her feet on top of his, began to sway her back and forth. Then her Uncle Jim did the same. Everyone who was watching grew teary-eyed.

We all danced the night away and had the time of our lives.

At one point, while on the dance floor, I remember looking up and thanking God for a beautiful and amazing day.

Chapter 22

Back to Florida

When we returned to Florida on July 21, a very dear friend of Lish's came to help and give a measure of normalcy to her life.

Aubrey —a slip of a girl, beautiful inside and out—had been friends with Lish since junior high school. She pitched right in doing everything and anything she could to help us. She was extremely good with Lish. She provided encouragement, helped feed her, changed, bathed, dressed and primped her.

The other children loved Aubrey too. When she wasn't helping with Lish, she was playing with them. Janine and I were so grateful for everything she did. We would tell Lish that a good friend stays with you in good times and in bad. Aubrey really was a true friend, the kind who leaves footprints on your heart.

Early that August, we called Jane—our newfound friend from the makeup counter who plays Bell—and made arrangements to meet her at the Magic Kingdom. We bought a ticket for Aubrey and Lish's sister, Alexis.

Jane was permitted to get Lish, Janine, and I in for free!

We spent the most magical day at the park, laughing, talking, eating and riding. The employees did so much to accommodate Lish in her wheelchair. They assisted us when needed, slowed down rides if possible, and treated us all like celebrities.

We made memories that day to last a lifetime.

Therapy continued at Celebration Hospital, Florida. Lish's therapists worked diligently with her, and she made substantial progress.

The therapists continued with routine Kinesio Taping and showed us how to apply the tape if it came off while Lish was asleep or if she removed it.

Several of the therapists made the same remark: "This kind of progress isn't usually what we see with such a severe injury."

The report gave all of us a boost.

Prayers never stopped, therapy continued, and the work never ended.

Sadly, we were forced to return to Pennsylvania so her siblings could return to school. It was a somber day when we had to say good-bye to Jamie, Brunella and Christina. They told us—like her therapists did at the SSBI Unit—that they wanted to see her again and looked forward to that visit.

Chapter 23

Home Again

Lish started outpatient therapy on August 26 at HealthSouth, a rehabilitation facility near our house outside Pittsburgh. Because the center sits only about 10 minutes away, she stayed with Jim and me from Monday through Thursday.

Her parents and siblings lived about an hour away. For that reason, everyone agreed the arrangement was for the best, largely because it would enable her to devote much-needed time to the other children and she was confident we would take good care of Lish.

When Lish started at HealthSouth, she continued having trouble staying awake. Her high dosage of Keppra, the anti-seizure medication, kept her fatigued. Her physical rehabilitation physician agreed to immediately lower the dose from 2500 mg per day to 2000 mg daily and said that after one month it could be cut to 1500 mg.

The change in dosage made a huge difference. Lish was more awake and alert for all of her therapies. As a result, she made steady progress.

Just like at the hospital in Florida, Lish loved the therapists at HealthSouth. The dedicated and skilled team—physical therapists Dale, Susan, and Amy; occupational therapist, Sandy; and speech therapist, Janice—seemed to enjoy working with her as well.

They too were given nicknames: Dale became "Estabon," and Amy was dubbed, "Awesome Amy." Lish also provided each of the others with unique nicknames as well.

By the middle of August, Lish was able to control her bladder much better and stay dry most of the day. We did have the occasional flood that penetrated pads, sheets and even the sofa. Still, things were much improved.

Most nights, however, she remained incontinent. It was something how she managed to soak through so many pads, even limiting fluids early in the evening.

She was attempting to feed herself, although the task remained difficult because her tremors persisted. We praised every little success she had. She would tell us, "it makes me so happy to have someone tell me how good I am doing."

She would try to write, although that proved to be tough, too. "It looks like crap," she would quip.

She was right.

Walking remained a challenge because she would tend to lean backwards. It took everything we and her other caregivers had to keep her going forward. When corrected, she insisted she was doing it the right way.

"Perception is reality," I told her. The perception she was standing straight made it hard on everyone. Her constant disagreeing and need for correction and reinforcement was draining as well.

September flew by, and Lish continued to achieve slow, steady progress.

Her therapists put her on the auto-ambulator every Thursday. The machine supported her and did 50 percent of the work. Lish managed to walk one mile with relatively few stops. It was now her left foot that was the problem, tripping up the machine at intervals.

The other two days at therapy involved walking around the gym with her walker and transferring from a sitting position to a standing one and then reversing the process.

Lish was able to stand for four minutes with someone at the ready in case she lost her balance.

In occupational therapy, Sandy introduced Lish to the Interactive Metronome. The goals for her were to improve coordination, balance, focus, and attention. The program provided a structured process that challenged Lish to synchronize a range of hand and foot exercises to a precise computer-generated tone heard through headphones.

If Lish moved too soon or too late, a red or yellow light flashed. A green light meant she matched with the beat.

When she started, she saw more red lights than anything else. But her determination didn't wane. She did what was asked of her—most of the time with a smile.

Other patients and caregivers always commented on that smile. When they told us they thought she was doing better, we smiled as well.

Lish's personality and sense of humor stayed intact. She was her old bubbly self, which we were so very grateful for. But, she struggled with her memory.

Her memory deficits were determined by tests given by her speech therapist, Janice. The results weren't always encouraging. Lish remained easily distracted, always chatting and saying humorous things, just like the Lish everyone loved and enjoyed being around prior to the dreadful day of the accident.

While it was more important for her now to concentrate, it just wasn't possible at times.

On October 6, Jim and I were in the kitchen and looked at Lish. There she sat on the sofa, with her computer on her lap and pink cell phone pressed against her ear. Eight months post accident and this is what we saw. The picture was nothing like the one the doctors had painted. God is so good and does answer prayers, we thought. We hugged each other and thanked Him again for this giant step forward.

Every Monday, Wednesday, and Thursday followed the same routine. I woke at 7 A.M., showered and dressed. By then it was time to wake Lish and get her ready. She still required assistance with bathing and grooming but was beginning to help dress and undress herself.

It was a challenge to eat breakfast and get out the door by 8:30 A.M.

Jim drove a school bus and was just getting in the door at that time. As soon as he walked in, he turned around and took us to HealthSouth.

As soon as we arrived at the facility, I would walk in and grab a wheelchair. Jim and I then helped Lish into the wheelchair, giving her constant cues. "Back up until you feel the chair with the back of your legs," we'd say. "Bend down. Reach with your hands, and slowly lower yourself." I had instructed my patients the same way over the years I worked, and now I was doing the same with Lish. I repeated it with each transfer, hoping it would sink in.

Then, we'd race down the quarter-mile hallway to the gym. Three hours later, we headed back to the car and to home for lunch.

After this morning routine, the three of us were exhausted.

Lish would talk on her phone or play a game on the computer while Jim and I took a short nap. Before we knew it, it was time for me to start supper, and Jim to return to his bus run. In the time between the nap, work, and dinner, Jim and I dealt with constant trips to the bathroom with Lish.

The job of assisting with the shower, shampoo, and hair straightening was up to me. And, just when I thought the laundry was done, along came another load.

This routine continued weekly until the middle of December.

Some days were up and others down, but there were more ups. Lish would ask her therapists at the end of each session, "Was I a 10?" If they said she was, her smile lit up the room. She could hardly wait to tell her pap and her mom.

Lish reached a major milestone on December 7 when she took one and a half steps in therapy without her walker.

As a family, we were thrilled. Her therapists were elated as well. It was a tiny step, but a huge accomplishment to witness her taking her first step without a walker. We felt like our girl was going to walk one day.

Not long after the monumental occasion, we bid Lish's therapists goodbye and prepared to make our way back to Florida for Christmas.

Chapter 24

Grandma Will Do Anything

One day, while Lish was still going through her therapy sessions, I read an article stating Keppra could contribute to tremors and balance problems. Since these were two big problems Lish was having, I was intent on having the dosage of this medication decreased.

Dr. Burton, who specialized in motion disorders, agreed it was time to begin tapering off the medication. He said he would be in touch with Lish's physical rehabilitation doctor to see if she agreed.

A few days later, on a Sunday morning, I went into a local coffee shop and saw a woman I thought was Dr. Leslie—Lish's primary care physician. She was wearing a Steelers shirt and Steelers earrings, so I asked if she was going to the game. She said she wasn't but added she planned to go the following week.

I later discovered the Steelers weren't even playing at home the day I approached this woman.

She went along with me, acting as if she knew who I was. I apologized for asking, but told her I was determined to get Lish off the Keppra. So, I proceeded to ask, if in her medical opinion, it would be okay to decrease the medication by 250 mg.

The woman seemed to think for a moment and then replied, "I don't think you should do that." So, I thanked her and apologized again for bothering her on her day off.

Then I went to Marshall's to return a pair of shoes I bought the day before. A petite woman who was waiting in line at the return register asked if I was returning something also. She said: "Don't you remember me? I saw you yesterday. I'm 'Dr. Leslie.'"

I wondered if I was losing my mind. After telling the doctor what I'd done, we laughed so hard.

I told her, "I guess that proves I'll do anything to get her off that medicine, even ask strangers."

When I shared with Lish, Janine, and the rest of the family what I'd done, they cracked up. It became the "I'll-do-anything-to-get-Lish-off-of-Keppra" story.

On December 8, Janine took Lish to see her physical rehabilitation doctor.

Lish relayed the story about me asking a stranger about reducing her Keppra. She then told the doctor she wanted off the medication because it was making her too tired.

The doctor agreed, but warned Lish and her mom that she might have a seizure. She explained to Janine and Lish the warning signs and said she needed to go to the hospital immediately if a seizure occurred.

She told Lish she thought she might have a seizure, but hoped Lish would ' prove her wrong.'

Janine and her family and Jimmy and his family spent Christmas with us in Florida. John and Monica weren't able to make it.

Having so much family around was a welcome change for Lish and those of us who regularly took care of her. We had sun, blue skies, and warm temperatures—a pleasant change.

Every day, we continued to work with Lish on walking. She insisted we count every step and tell her how many she had taken. Her gait was far from fluid and could be better described as "robotic."

One of us stood in front of Lish and the other close behind to prevent her from falling. Even though she lost her balance frequently, she was increasing her steps by one or two each day. This was what all of us had prayed for but weren't sure we'd ever see.

Come December, Lish's Keppra dose had been reduced significantly, and by New Year's Day, she was off the drug completely.

On December 17 she was still only able to take one and a half steps on her own. But, one week later she took 12 steps.

Each week, she took several more steps and lost her balance a little less frequently. Her gait was awkward, but she was walking. Praise God. Was this the walking miracle we were waiting for?

When we returned to therapy after the holidays, we couldn't wait for Lish to show off for her therapists. All of them, including the aides, secretaries, and even other patients and their families, were as thrilled as we were to see the tremendous progress she made.

Amy began working with Lish at this time, walking her around the gym. She would time her and count the number of times she lost her balance.

Each of the therapists knew just where to place their hands, so if she would fall forward or backwards, they could control her.

They agreed it would be best if Lish continued to use her walker at home.

Some days were better than others, but her gait just wasn't fluid. It still had a robotic quality. The fact that she was walking at all, however, was awesome.

Everyone wondered if it was a coincidence that Lish was able to start walking when she stopped taking her anti-seizure medication, or if it was in God's plan for her to begin walking at that time.

Over the next several months, Lish gained added proficiency using her walker.

Wherever she walked, we stayed close by.

Her therapists instructed us not to touch her when she had the walker. They felt it would send a message to her brain that she didn't need to maintain her balance. This was difficult for us. The last thing we wanted was for Lish to fall and injure herself.

In occupational therapy, Sandy had Lish working with the Interactive Metronome on a regular basis. Lish continually improved by decreasing her time and increasing her accuracy. More green lights started to appear.

One day, Jim was with her at therapy. He was watching her and thought, "That doesn't look too hard." The therapist asked if he would like to try it. Thinking it was easy, he soon learned otherwise. His score was far below Lish's. She really enjoyed beating her pap and they both had a good laugh about it.

The speech therapist, Janice, worked with Lish on language and thought processing (comprehension, retention, and organization). She would read her a story and then ask her questions about what she had just read. I would silently try to answer the questions and had a lot of problems recalling all of the details Lish was expected to remember.

I was shocked to find out the readings were at a fifth-grade level.

Chapter 25

A Forgotten Day

During that first year of healing, Lish spoke quite often about not remembering her 19th birthday. Everyone wanted to be sure she not only remembered her 20th, but that she really enjoyed it.

Monica planned to have a sleepover birthday party for Lish at her home. She sent out e-mail invites to the girls Lish requested be invited. Since most of her friends were away at college, we feared not many would come, but didn't share this concern with Lish.

We were pleasantly surprised to have 12 girls show up.

As we sat there watching our girl talking, laughing and joking around, it made everybody's heart overflow with joy.

Lish opened her cards with those darn trembling hands. But instead of getting frustrated and giving up, she made a joke and kept on trying. We admired her determination and persistence.

Lish told everyone she will never forget her 20th birthday and neither will anyone who was there.

Chapter 26

We Pray for What We Want,
but God Gives Us What We Need

Lish woke up one morning looking so sad.

"I'm so bummed out," she said. "It really stinks that I can't remember my 19th birthday or the accident."

Her usual smile was gone. Her eyes were sad and filled with tears. I immediately took her into my arms and hugged her tightly. I told her how far she had come and how good God had been to her and to all who love her as well.

She was starting to grasp all she had lost from the accident.

"If only I could go back," she said.

"If only I had buckled up that day," she said.

"Why didn't I do it?"

"If I could turn back time," I quipped. Lish then started singing the lyrics to that Cher classic.

We all have a "take-back" moment in our lives; some of us, more than one, I told her.

I then related to her one of my take-back moments that occurred many years ago. Lish listened, as I shared my story:

"I had just gotten home from working the daylight shift at the hospital. There was dinner to make, a scout meeting, and dance practice to get to. But first, the newspapers had to be delivered. The weather was terrible, pouring down rain and my son—the paperboy— was sick on the sofa. I decided it was best to drive the paper route with your uncle and your mom, so as not to have soaked papers or soaked children. I loaded your uncle John into his car seat, and your mom hopped into the front seat next to me. She was talking away, just like you do. I put the car in reverse and saw a white thing in my rearview mirror, but that didn't stop me from pressing the accelerator even harder. It was at that moment I realized what I had done. I had just backed through the garage door."

Looking back, that moment was nothing compared to what my family was dealing with now. Lish couldn't be fixed as easily as a garage door. Yet at that time, I thought it was the worst day of my life.

As a family, we all wished we could go back to the day of the accident. We would make sure Lish wasn't so rushed for her Spanish test, make sure her seatbelt was fastened securely, and remove the ice from the road. Unfortunately, life doesn't always allow "do-overs."

No one ever mentioned the seat belt issue during her critical stages. As I said, it really was like the elephant in the room. It loomed over everyone's thoughts, but who could talk about it? Everyone thought, if she had her seat belt on, she most likely would have been spared the severe head trauma she sustained.

Much later in her recovery, she often expressed remorse for not wearing her seat belt. She would ask me, "Why didn't I buckle up?" She made it a point of asking friends, "Do you wear your seatbelt?"

Chapter 27

Messed Up Smile

Early one frigid Saturday morning near the end of February 2010, Janine called to say Lish fell in the kitchen. She had gotten up to go to the bathroom and didn't want to bother her mom. She tripped, fell forward with her walker and broke off one of her front teeth and chipped two others. She bit her bottom lip, but Janine didn't think she needed stitches.

Jim and I again rushed over to Janine's home, where a police car and an ambulance were already in the driveway. Inside, the EMTs were placing Lish on a stretcher. She was apologizing for what had happened as she covered her mouth. She said how terrible she felt about the entire incident.

After several hours in the emergency room, the doctor informed Lish, Janine, and I that Lish's CT scan remained unchanged. The doctor also put a bonding compound on her teeth and advised her to see a dentist immediately.

Janine called her brother Jimmy to see if he could find her dentist's number to call and set up an appointment as soon as possible. While Jimmy was doing that, he saw his neighbor going out for the paper. He ran out and asked the man, who happened to be a dentist, if he would be able to see Lish.

This wonderful man agreed to meet us at his office on Saturday (which was his day off) and did wonders. It was hard to believe, but after two hours of work, Lish had her smile back.

Like the time Lish had her swearing jag, I rode with her again after her fall, in the back of the ambulance on the way to the hospital.

I had started talking with the EMT after he finished his paperwork. He said he remembered Lish from the day of the accident. It was supposed to be his day off, but when he heard the call go out over the radio, he decided to go to the scene of the accident anyway. This was the nurse who helped save Lish's life. I was face to face with him.

This EMT's primary job is working in the emergency room at two local hospitals. But he also works for the fire department two days a week because he loves his work so much.

His critical-care training proved invaluable for Lish. He recalled that after the firemen extricated her from her car, he and two other EMTs rode with her, working to help her, while a fireman drove the ambulance.

For whatever reason, he said, they were told on the way to the accident that they didn't need to go. They were told no one was in the car. But, as he explained to me, he just felt he had to go—and thank God he did.

I told him I didn't know if he believed in miracles, but that I believe that is exactly the word that best describes Lish. She is a "miracle."

He replied, "She most definitely is."

He said the emergency crew tried to keep informed about Lish's progress, and that with each achievement she makes, they continue to be amazed.

That's when I asked if it would be possible to meet with the first responders to thank them for all they had done.

We chose the date and set up a meeting. About a dozen men and one woman (firefighters and EMTs) showed up. Most, in some way, had been responsible for getting Lish out of her car and ultimately to AGH the morning of her accident.

A few hadn't been on duty that day, but wanted to hear Lish's story, if for no other reason than to better understand the importance of what they do, most of them on a strictly volunteer basis.

Lish looked beautiful the day of the meeting. She walked in with her walker. Grown men were brought to tears.

"We didn't think you were going to live," one fireman said.

"A lot of guys had doubts that you would make it," another said.

Those involved with the rescue, even more so than being surprised, said they were overjoyed to see that she defied the odds.

"It was really inspiring when they told us you had taken a few steps on your own," one of them told Lish.

She then stood up with me close by her side and demonstrated to them what she was able to do. She took several steps without her walker.

Applause rang out and hugs followed.

Lish said, "Now we have another story to tell everyone, grandma."

I told her, "Thanks, but we have enough stories."

I remind myself tomorrow is another day. Hopefully, no more falls.

Chapter 28

Continued Recovery

During March and April, Lish continued on her journey to recovery.

Her long- and short-term memory were better than mine. I would tell my friends this, and they would laugh.

Lish's voice grew stronger and easier to understand. Still, when she spoke on the telephone, most people had difficulty understanding her.

She was reading, texting, and communicating with family and friends on Facebook. This presented an occasional problem in terms of what Lish would choose to share with others. But with some guidance, Lish started to understand what was appropriate and what wasn't.

Finally, Lish took her fifth and final swallow test and was cleared to drink liquids. The test results showed she was no longer aspirating, meaning she could have the Starbucks Strawberry and Cream Frappachino she loved so much, minus the thickener.

She was cleared to eat anything, although we continued to cut her food into small pieces. She had a tendency to put large portions of food into her mouth; it was her altered perception.

She would disagree with us that the pieces were small, but this too passed in time.

The incontinence was under control during the day, with a few accidents at night. She was able to get up and down at night and go to the bathroom, requiring only supervision.

She could take 32 steps unassisted by the end of April but still struggled with fine motor control. Everyone was optimistic that this would continue to improve.

Chapter 29

People Stare

As a family, we tried to get Lish out of the house as much as possible—to the mall to shop or to a restaurant for dinner.

The person walking behind her was always aware of those watching us. Wherever we went, people would stare.

Lish smiled at everyone. It was the Lish we knew before the accident. Sometimes people would return the smile; sometimes they would look and quickly glance away. Sometimes, we could see pity in their eyes.

It's not common to see a young girl slowly pushing a walker. I'm sure some wondered: "What's her story? Why is she using a walker? What's wrong with her?"

Lish's smile would often engage some individuals who would then talk to her and comment, "What a beautiful smile you have." She would then politely reply, "Thank you."

Those haunting words, "she'll never be 100%" float in and out of my mind at times. Then I think, not one of us is really 100%—only God.

Don't we all have the feeling of imperfection or inadequacy at one time or another? That pimple on our face feels like a neon sign drawing attention. Those extra pounds we just can't lose make us uncomfortable. It doesn't have to be a physical thing; it could be the feeling of being unworthy.

I wanted to say—no, I wanted to shout—to everyone: "If you only knew where we were one year ago. If you only knew what the doctors were telling us. If you only knew she was in a coma for one month; if you only knew the power of prayer and what an awesome and caring God we have."

It turned out to be harsh winter in Pittsburgh that year. We had an above-average level of snowfall and below normal temperatures.

Lish continued to stay with Jim and me Sunday through Thursday and attend therapy every Monday, Wednesday, and Thursday. If she was in good spirits, she would work hard throughout all of her therapy sessions. If she was feeling down, it was a struggle. "Why? Why? Why?" she would often say. Then she would say, "Pardon my French, but this really stinks." She longed to be independent again.

I would tell Lish, "You must try your best. My back is breaking."

She would then apologize and say she would work harder, and we would hug.

"I don't know why I am being such a moose," she would say.

Many tears flowed during these long, dreary months.

Lish wanted her phone and computer constantly. I encouraged her to read something—a magazine, newspaper, a few chapters in a book, anything.

"It will help with your comprehension," I told her.

It became a struggle at times.

Lish joined me, her aunt Lora and Monica, and cousin Brooke in forming a book club. We decided to read *The Last Song*, by Nicholas Sparks.

We promised Lish that if she read the book, she could choose the restaurant we would eat at after seeing the movie.

We thought it would give her a goal and something fun to look forward to.

She kept saying, "I want to see the movie first." No one gave in. We insisted she read the book.

It took her about five weeks to finish it. Then the big day came. Needless to say, we were all excited. We ate at Panera Bread and then went to see the movie.

We were anxious to hear what Lish had to say.

After leaving the theater, we asked her what she thought. She said, "I liked the book better." She then proceeded to recall five facts that were in the book but not in the movie.

We were amazed she could recall the details from the book. It was also encouraging to know she could identify the missing scenes.

I wondered if her attention and comprehension were getting better.

During these dreary months, Lish progressed in physical therapy to the point of being able to walk around the gym with contact guard assist from her therapists, Amy and Dale. "Contact guard assist" meant that Lish's therapists would place one hand in front of her right shoulder and one hand on her left hip to assist her as she walked.

On occasion, she lost her balance, but Amy and Dale were able to stabilize her. Her gait wasn't as fluid as it should be. It continued to look awkward and stiff.

Lish would walk on the auto-ambulator about one mile, occasionally stopping when she didn't lift her left foot high enough. The therapists were so patient in resetting the device and encouraging Lish. They knew how much she enjoyed music, so they put the radio on and tuned into her favorite channel. She would sing along as she walked. One thing she never seemed to forget were the lyrics to the music she liked.

On a return visit in March to see Dr. Burton, the motion specialist, I asked if there was a medication to help make Lish's gait more fluid. He immediately responded that there were several she could try. After he spoke of several medications and their side effects, he suggested we begin with a very low dose of Baclofen.

Dr. Burton explained that a delicate balance existed between decreasing the rigid muscle tone in her legs to make motion more fluid, but not decreasing the muscle tone so much that she would fall. After two weeks on the medications, we noticed her gait becoming less robotic and more fluid. It was far from normal, but she was on her own two feet and she was "walking."

Speech therapy still continued to be a challenge at times, especially when Janice, the speech therapist, gave Lish a test. She would place colored chips, of various sizes and shapes, on the table in front of Lish and proceed to give commands: "Place the blue circle on the red square. Place the small white square in front of the yellow circle." This comprised 75 questions.

I would sit behind Lish in the small windowless room, curious how she was doing.

Then came the final 25 questions, the "tricky ones."

Janice would tell Lish, "Each direction stands alone." She would then say, "If you haven't touched the red square, touch the white circle."

Lish would sit and say, "I'm not going to touch anything." She knew she had touched the red square during the previous questioning. In her mind, she couldn't grasp the concept that each direction now stood alone and nothing she had done previously mattered.

I joked with her: "The next time you take the test, I will cough when it comes to that part of the exam. Then you will understand what Janice means."

We would chuckle.

Another exercise Janice did was to read an article and then question Lish. "What was the man's name, how old was he, where did he live?"

I would sit there trying to recall the details. Then Lish would say, "How many did you miss, grandma?" Usually, I missed more than she did. This too provided for some laughter.

They say laughter is great medicine and both Lish and I agreed. It often helped to lighten the mood.

In occupational therapy, Lish still had difficulty with activities involving fine motor control, but this was improving as well. She would work on placing clothes pins on a rod and removing them using only her fingertips. Stacking cones and removing them was another exercise she practiced. She would try to write, but would say, "It still looks like crap." Even with a special weighted pen, the letters were up and down and difficult to read. She would try to steady her right hand with her left, but that did little.

Lish did enjoy working on the Metronome. Over time, she made significant improvements.

Chapter 30

Time for a Change

Days turned into weeks, and weeks into months. The world around us was beginning to wake up. The first sign of buds on the trees and flowers in the garden were a welcome sight. Spring was in full swing. After such a harsh winter, it made everyone happy and brought a smile to our faces.

Lish continued to work diligently in therapy and at home. I started having her make a simple lunch, such as a sandwich. She would then clean up and put things away. She was also able to go to the bathroom by herself, with the aid of only her walker.

She preferred a bath to a shower, so I watched her getting in and out of the tub. She was able to shave herself using the razor with the soap surrounding the blade. Through trials that often resulted in cuts, we found this approach to be the best for her. She required some assistance shampooing her long dark hair.

Lish was able to use a hot iron to straighten most of her hair. However, I asked her to wear long gloves to protect her from burns, and I made sure to sit right next to her. These were all huge accomplishments. Lish would say on occasion, "I can't wait to show those doctors what I can do."

On June 3, Lish had an appointment with her physical rehabilitation doctor. Her mom and I went with her. The doctor was so pleased with all the progress she had made.

Since the insurance company had terminated her therapy, the doctor said, "It's up to you now." She gave the approval for Lish to take one class at a community college. Lish argued that she wanted to take three classes and attend South Eastern University in Florida on a full time basis. After much discussion, and many tears, Lish agreed to do as her doctor

It Only Took a Moment

recommended. She told Lish, "I want to set you up for success, not failure."

The doctor provided us with a list of accommodations the school would need to make for Lish. They included giving her a copy of the notes as she was unable to write legibly, permitting her to have more time to take a test, and providing a tutor if necessary.

A month after Lish had been discharged from the SSBI unit, both the doctor's office and the SSBI unit moved to UPMC Mercy Hospital in Pittsburgh. After meeting with her doctors, Janine, Lish, and I took the opportunity to visit the staff members who had worked with Lish. It had been 13 months since they had seen her. Entering the brain injury unit and seeing the other families and patients was difficult.

The staff members on duty that day remembered Lish and were so happy to see her and the progress she had made.

When Lish saw Kim, her first physical therapist, she put her arms around her and apologized. "My mom and grandma told me I wasn't very nice to you," she said.

Kim told her that was not her, but the injury, and that she was so glad Lish came back to see everyone. Kim and the rest of the staff told Lish to continue the good work and encouraged her to stop by again to share the progress she was making.

Janine's other three children finished their school year on June 4. The very next day, Janine and her children were on a flight to Florida. The plan was to spend the summer at our home.

Jim and I arrived several days later. Fearful Lish would lose ground not being in a structured therapy program, we devised

159

one of our own. We went to water aerobics on Tuesday, Thursday, and Saturday mornings. The other days, Jim took her to the gym, where she rode a reclining bicycle, walked on the treadmill, and did sit ups.

Wow!—a treadmill without a harness and robotic legs. Lish's pap worked right alongside her. He said, "I was getting so tired, but didn't want to quit for fear she would want to quit."

Lish was able to get up in the morning and get dressed on her own. She then found her pap and told him that she was ready to begin with her work out whenever he was ready. We didn't know who was happier to report how she did when they got back, her pap or Lish. As soon as they returned home, they would outtalk one another saying how many miles she biked or how far she walked on the treadmill.

Janine and I felt it was time for the next step. We felt she was depending too much on her walker. It was good to have when out and about, but we knew she was able to walk inside without the device, provided there was close supervision. Janine went to the store and purchased a bike helmet, knee pads, and elbow pads. Lish was then free to move about in the home all by herself. We instructed her on the proper way to fall and moved every object out of her way. Everyone still watched her closely, however. Even her younger siblings helped to keep an eye on her.

It was Lish's first step at independence.

"I feel free," she said.

Her gait was less robotic, but she could only move about the house very slowly. The doctor said it was OK to increase the Baclofen in tiny amounts to improve her gait. This we did.

It took a lot of fine tuning but eventually she was walking a little faster, but still not smoothly.

Chapter 31

Back to School

On June 14, Lish had an appointment to meet the disability director at Valencia Community College in Kissimmee, Florida. He was a very friendly and helpful man. Lish told him she wanted to begin the summer session. He told her the session began in one week and explained the process that would need to unfold before she could attend.

She needed to fill out the on-line application and obtain her transcripts from both her high school and community college. He then said it would take three to five business days to process an application. She still insisted; this is what she wanted to do.

The disability director at Valencia asked Lish what her future plans were. She told him that after one semester there, she wanted to transfer to South Eastern University in Florida. He informed her he would check with them to see if they accepted the courses she had already taken and what future courses they would take for credit. A few tears streamed down her cheeks. He continued to be very kind and helpful.

"I'm not saying you can't do it," he said "It will just be very difficult to get everything done in the short time frame."

Lish then said, "But I want to start at South Eastern this fall." Janine and I looked at each other. "That is what she thinks is possible," we said to each other. The disability director did not discourage her, but said, "Let's just take one step at a time. I'm sure you'll get there."

The director spoke with us about auditing a class (attending a class without registering for credit) versus taking a credit course. He explained that he thought it would be best to take a class, and if after two weeks Lish found it too difficult, she could then convert the course into an audit class. Lish, Janine, and I were all in agreement to this plan.

Lish decided to take Speech or Spanish for her first class. The director checked and said she had met the language requirements. He also said the Speech professor was very kind and would offer a good start for her. Lish agreed and the decision was made. Classes would be held on Tuesdays and Thursdays from 2:30 P.M. to 3:30 P.M.

Janine then handed the director a letter from Lish's doctor that detailed all of the accommodations she required for class. He assured us that the speech professor would comply and do everything necessary to assist Lish in being successful.

With the paperwork and school handbook, we left his office. Lish had the saddest look on her face. The 25-minute ride home was very quiet. Lish just didn't want to talk much.

Her doctor, her parents, grandparents, and now the director at the school, told her it was going to take time; something she didn't want to hear.

The next week was one of Lish's most down and out weeks. She cried at anything and didn't want to do anything or go anywhere. Little by little, the severity of the accident was sinking in, but the visit to the community college brought it all to light.

Things weren't going to be the way they were prior to the accident. She wasn't able to get into her car and drive herself to school. In her heart, she wanted to return to school right where she had left off, but since the injury, that was not going to be possible.

Everyone trudged through, pulling her along. We continued to have her do her exercises and get her out as much as we could.

We called a family meeting. I said, "Lish, I just can't pull you anymore, my back is sore."

I quoted something I heard Oprah say on one of her shows: "The more we are thankful for what we have, the more we have to be thankful for."

We then told her how very far she had come and how much further, with God's assistance, she could still go.

"No one is saying you can never attend South Eastern University, just not now," I said. More tears and hugs followed.

Exactly one week later, Lish got up, brushed her teeth and put on her exercise clothes. She then walked out with her helmet on to find her pap.

"I'm ready to go to the gym when you are pap," she said. We never saw him move so quickly. Off they went laughing and talking.

Most days after that, she was happy to work out and go into the pool. What a difference this made for us. No more dragging and pulling.

Chapter 32

It's Not That Important

Ever since our life changing event, I have learned a very valuable life lesson: Put everything into proper perspective and weight how important it is.

Prior to the accident, I would fret about everything. When company was coming, everything had to be perfect. The house, the food, the conversation, all had to be just so. Nothing could be out of place. If the meal I prepared wasn't up to my expectation, I was a mess.

While driving down the highway and someone cuts you off, or in a grocery store some rude person steps in front of you, our initial reaction may be to get upset. But, how important is it?

Now, I look at all these things that come my way in a different light. Instead of being preoccupied with insignificant inconveniences that sometimes occur, I just say to myself, "How important is it?"

So far, nothing has proven to be that important. If the house isn't spotless, the food isn't perfect, if an event didn't go as planned, how important was it? In the whole scheme of things, one's health is the most important. If we could all learn this lesson before a tragedy strikes us.

Every time I listen to the news and hear about an auto accident, or see a helicopter fly overhead, my heart is sad. I think about the patient and his or her family and feel for the difficult journey of pain and emotions they are about to experience.

This truly has been one of the most difficult periods of my life. At one time, many years earlier in my life, I thought going back to work after being away for 12 years was physically and emotionally draining and difficult. It seemed that everything had changed since I last worked. I felt like I was starting over. Medicine is a very rapidly changing career. From the time I had left, until I returned, I said the only thing that didn't change was the way we took someone's blood pressure. Medications, treatments, and care delivery systems had all changed. Computers were introduced and they were so foreign to me.

When my instructor spoke about a hard drive and a floppy disc I thought, "What the heck is she talking about?"

I pulled out of the parking lot of the hospital every day wondering how I would ever catch up. How would I ever learn all the new technology that was introduced since I last worked?

Days, weeks, and months passed. My confidence increased and so did my knowledge.

Months turned into years, and before I knew it, I was orienting new nurses to the unit. Remembering how difficult it was for me, I always tried to be kind and encouraging.

Strange, how whatever stage in life, we think it can't get any worse. Raising children is by far one of the most difficult jobs anyone can do. Working outside the home adds another challenge. Having to experience one's own physical discomfort or financial hardship can be depressing. But dealing with a loved one with a traumatic brain injury is truly a life altering event.

I will never look at things in life the same way again.

Over the years, I heard my mom say, "If you have your health, you have everything." I used to think, "Sure mom." Now I realize how very wise she was.

Chapter 33

Almost Full-Circle

August 24 was the much anticipated day. Lish was planning for weeks what she would wear, how she would fix her hair and asked her mom to apply her makeup. She was beginning to master this task, but sometimes used a heavy hand and put on too much. Lish said, "I don't want to look like a clown on my first day, so I want you to do it, mom."

Lish was up, bathed, and dressed by 10A.M. Into the living room she walked with her backpack on and that wonderful smile we all loved. She said, "I'm all ready except for my makeup."

I said, "Lish, you have plenty of time."

She replied, "I know grandma, but I don't want to be late my first day."

She had nicknames for everything and everyone. Her wheelchair was named "Pablo," her walker, "Junior," and her cane, "Leo." Her friends decorated Junior with heart stickers. When we had Lish and Junior out, he attracted a lot of attention and questions like, "Where did you get such a fancy walker?" Lish would laugh and tell them her friends did the art work for her.

After lunch, Jim helped Janine load up Lish and Junior. We all hugged, kissed and told her to have a great day. I felt like I was sending my first born off to school for the first time.

Janine made the half hour trip, walked Lish into the building and attempted to orient her and point her in the direction of her classroom. Janine then went to pick up Alexis, Steven, and Anthony. By the time she had the children seated in her car, it was time to turn around and head back to pick up Lish.

All the while, Janine's mind was on Lish. "How was she doing? Was the professor nice? Were the other students kind to her?"

Then, as Janine arrived at the college, she saw Lish emerge from the classroom. A huge smile was on her face and she couldn't wait to share her experience. With excitement, she said: "My professor is so sweet, and even though the other classmates didn't sit by me, they seemed nice."

Janine tried to talk more with Lish, but the other children wanted to tell about their days as well.

Jim and I could hardly wait to see Lish. She looked happy, and that was all I cared about.

After supper, we had a chance to catch up on her day. She informed us that her first speech was called a "Brown Bag Speech." She told us her professor said, "This first speech will help to get your feet wet and aquainted with different parts of a speech and different delivery techniques."

I once heard that giving a speech is one of a human beings most dreaded fears. It never seemed to faze Lish before, and it didn't now.

She worked diligently on that speech. We all were so please she was able to write it all on her own. When it came time to practice, that was a different story. She would stand up in front of us, begin to deliver the first line and forget the second. Over and over and over again she would begin and attempt to complete this four minute speech.

We all began laughing and were able to recite it by heart when the week of practice was over.

Lish signed up to be the first student to deliver her speech on September 21. She titled it, "A Positive Attitude."

It reads:

I believe that everyone has a specific purpose in life. I know that with a positive attitude, many things can be accomplished. So I am going to take you back to when I was in 6th grade.

I played volleyball for 6 years. I was always the encourager and I tried to focus on the positives. Regardless if we were down by a point or many points, I always would tell my teammates things like...we would get them next time or good try. I was the team captain for 2 of my years and believe my motivational skills help in this position.

I never could have expected what would occur on February 4, 2009. The day after my 19th birthday. I am using "Junior" for my next example.

So I was driving to a community college back in Pennsylvania when my car slid on black ice. I was in a terrible car accident. I was in a coma for 1 month. The doctors gave my loved ones little hope. They recommended I be put in a hospital and at best I would probably be in a vegetative state for life.

The doctors had even talked about removing my life support. Praise Jesus that my family didn't listen! I have had to relearn everything from eating, talking and just holding my head up. My whole situation kind of stinks at times but I don't let that get me down or upset. I just think about where I have come from and that is enough motivation for me to maintain my positive attitude and continue to press on forward.

Here is my speech book as a little token of hope towards my future. My goal is to graduate from Valencia and move on to a four year college. To be honest, after high school, I never wanted to go to a community college. I wanted to move away and go to a four year University. I did make the most of it and ended up on the Dean's list. I am now so thankful for the opportunity to just be back in school.

I know that the road is rough and that everyone wishes there were redos in life. Unfortunately there is not. I believe that everyone has a specific purpose in life but mine has yet to be fulfilled. With a positive attitude, many things will be accomplished. My positive attitude has helped me in surviving and getting by everyday life. I believe that with a positive attitude, I CANNOT BE STOPPED!!!!!!

This speech earned Lish an "A"—97 percent. She couldn't wait to call everyone and share her fabulous news.

The end of this story is yet to be known. Only God knows how far our girl will go, what wonderful things she will do, and how she will serve Him in the best possible way.

One thing is for sure: Our family and anyone who knows of Lish's story truly believe that ALL THINGS ARE POSSIBLE WITH GOD.

Looking Back

**Photos and Images
Along the Road to Recovery**

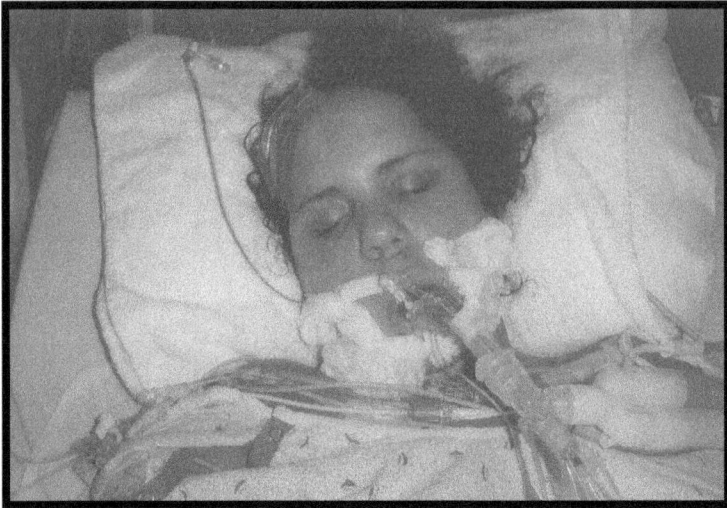

Lish in the trauma unit shortly after her accident.

Photo board with well wishes from family and friends.

Kim (physical therapist) helping Lish do the impossible—or so the doctors said.

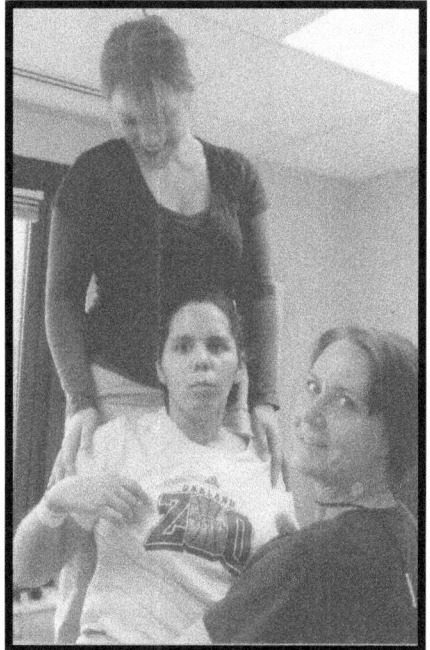

Lish with her physical therapists at the SSBI unit.

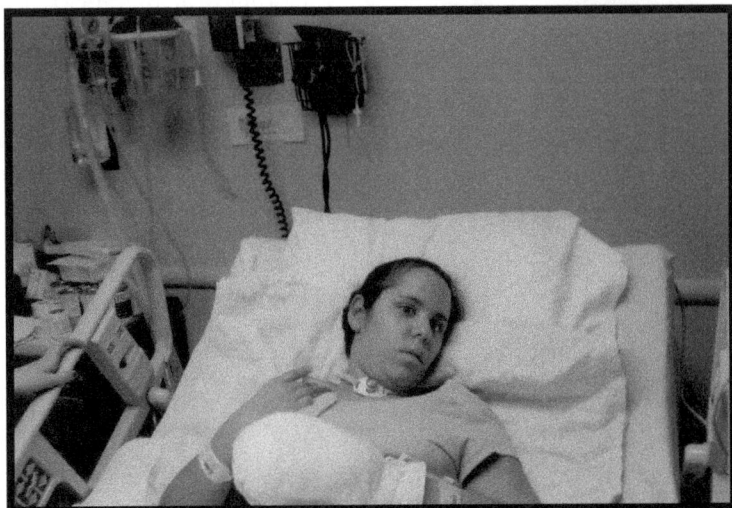

Lish at South Side Rehabilitation Unit.

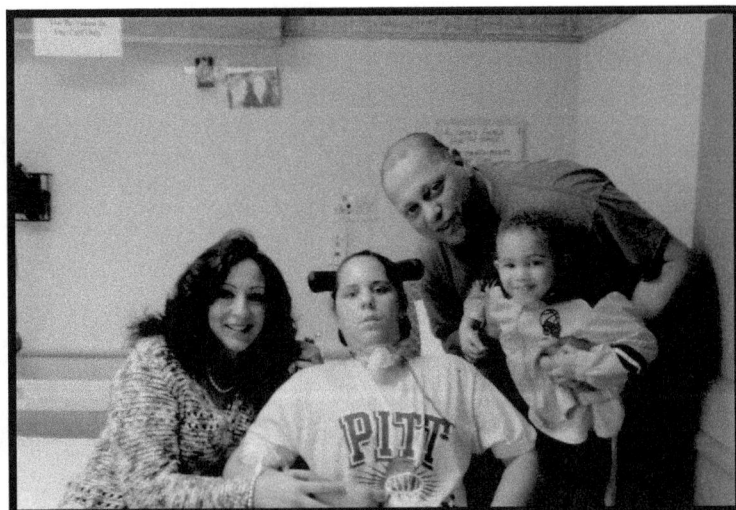

Mom, Dad (Stan), and brother Stosh visit with Lish during rehab.

Left to Right: Brooke, Brian, Steven, Lish, Alexis, Aubrey, Matt, Anthony, and Nicholas (Easter 2009)

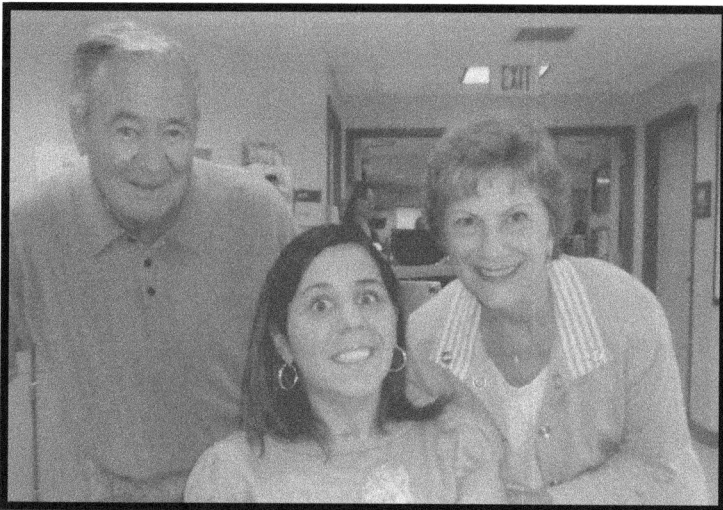

The day Pap, Lish, and Gram left rehab.

John and Monica's Wedding Day (our Christmas card).

Carol (Lora's Mom), Brooke, Monica, Lora, Regina, Lish, Janine, and Alexis.

Our special day at the Magic Kingdom.

"Brilliant Brunella" and Lish at Celebration Rehabilitation in Florida.

Lish's heroes—Economy Borough First Responders.

Lish with her BFF Grace.

Halloween Party 2010—Our Miracle Girl!